SWALEDALE & THE NORTH

Kirkby Stephen

Keld

9

Langthwaite

10

Reeth

Richmond

B6270

B6270

Sedbergh

7 Hawes

Aysgarth

3

West Burton

8

Leyburn

River Ure

Bedale

A684

Thirsk

WENSLEYDALE

Dent

Masham

A6108

A1

CENTRAL DALES

Hubberholme

6

Ingleton

Horton in Ribblesdale

Arncliffe

5

Kettlewell

Lofthouse

4

Clapham

Grassington

Pateley Bridge

A61

Ripon

1

Settle

3

Malham

2

B6265

HARROGATE & RIPON

A1(M)

Knaresborough

GATEWAY TO THE DALES

A65

2

Bolton Abbey

A59

Harrogate

B6451

Skipton

2

Keighley

Haworth

A629

Burnley

Blackburn

Preston

Durham

Darlington

Middlesbrough

Wakefield

Huddersfield

Rochdale

6 Walk start point

1 Cycle start point

2 Tour start point

D1380264

LEISURE GUIDE

Yorkshire Dales

Author: Mike Gerrard
Verifier and additional text: Chris Bagshaw
Managing Editor: David Popey
Project Management: Bookwork Creative Associates
Designers: Liz Baldin of Bookwork and Andrew Milne
Picture Library Manager: Ian Little
Picture Research: Liz Stacey and Michelle Aylott
Cartography provided by the Mapping Services Depart
Copy-editors: Marilynne Lanng of Bookwork and Pam
Internal Repro and Image Manipulation: Sarah Montg
Production: Rachel Davis

Produced by AA Publishing
© AA Media Limited 2007
Reprinted 2007, 2008
Updated and revised 2010

FLINTSHIRE SIR Y FFLINT	
C29 0000 0616 256	
ASKEWS & HOLT	29-Dec-2011
914.284	£9.99
MI	

Published by AA Publishing (a trading name of AA Media Limited, whose registered office is Fanum
House, Basing View, Basingstoke, Hampshire RG21 4EA; registered number 06112600).

This product includes mapping data licensed from the Ordnance Survey®
with the permission of the Controller of Her Majesty's Stationery Office.
© Crown Copyright 2011. All rights reserved. Licence number 100021153.

ISBN: 978-0-7495-6696-8
ISBN: 978-0-7495-6709-5 (SS)

A CIP catalogue record for this book is available from the British Library.

The contents of this book are believed correct at the time of printing. Nevertheless, the publishers
cannot be held responsible for any errors or omissions or for changes in the details given in this
book or for the consequences of any reliance on the information it provides. We have tried to ensure
accuracy in this book, but things do change and we would be grateful if readers would advise us of
any inaccuracies they may encounter. This does not affect your statutory rights.

We have taken all reasonable steps to ensure that the walks and cycle rides in this book are safe and
achievable by people with a realistic level of fitness. However, all outdoor activities involve a degree of
risk and the publishers accept no responsibility for any injuries caused to readers whilst following
these walks and cycle rides. For advice on walking and cycling in safety, see pages 16–17.

Some of the walks and cycle routes may appear in other AA books.

Visit AA Publishing at theAA.com/shop

Printed and bound in China by C&C

A04393

CONTENTS

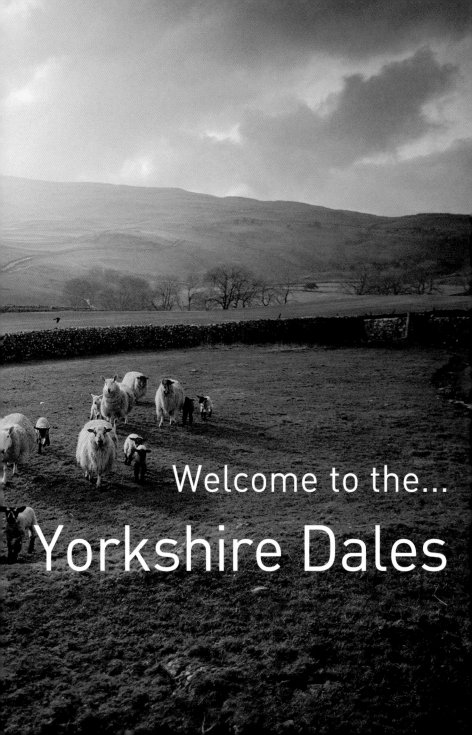

Welcome to the...
Yorkshire Dales

INTRODUCTION

With a huge National Park at its core, the Yorkshire Dales is a region of exquisite beauty, and a surprising amount of variety. In the southern region, Airedale and Wharfedale lead you out of the great West Yorkshire conurbation, fingers of moorland and secluded side valleys stretching into its heart. By the time you have travelled as far upstream as Skipton or Bolton Abbey, you know you are in the countryside proper – the roads get narrower, the hills get higher. As Upper Wharfedale stretches ahead of you so Upper Airedale becomes closed in, and in the mighty cliffs of Malham Cove and Gordale Scar you are left in no doubt that limestone has now replaced gritstone as the dominant bedrock.

The valleys and high fells were formed by shifts and faults in the earth's structure. When glacial ice swept down from the north, it carved the distinct U-shapes that are recognisable in Wensleydale, Swaledale and Wharfedale. The fertile upland landscape proved excellent for sheep farming – today the National Park logo is the head of a Swaledale tup (ram). Wool brought riches to the monks at Fountains and Jervaulx and Bolton priory, and prosperity to the market towns of Masham, Skipton, Richmond and Ripon. It was the raw material for the industrial growth of West Yorkshire, and the mill-owners built their spa playgrounds at Ilkley and Harrogate.

Sheep are still very important in the Dales, but their place in the local economy has been overtaken by tourism. The influx of visitors has brought fresh challenges to the region. In the 1950s the National Park was created to protect and enhance this unique landscape. Car parks and visitor centres were established at popular Dales sights, such as Aysgarth Falls, Malham and Grassington. Small-scale industry was encouraged and the scars of former mining and quarrying were protected for posterity. In the 1980s, tourism saved the region's last remaining railway, as the truly magnificent Leeds–Settle–Carlisle route was given due recognition as an attraction in its own right. Now thousands make the exciting journey through 14 tunnels and over 17 viaducts as it passes through the very core of the region.

Away from the honeypots you will still find solitude, maybe on the lonely heights above Swaledale, in a secret gill beneath looming Ingleborough, or amongst the heather moors of the south, where the Brontë sisters roamed. There are many quiet corners of the Dales to be found and treasured.

6   Walk start point

1   Cycle start point

2   Tour start point

8

1

Pennine Way

2

3

4

ESSENTIAL SIGHTS

Soak up the atmospheric ruined abbeys of Fountains or Jervaulx, both Cistercian monasteries founded in the 12th century...explore the fine 18th-century mansion of Newby Hall, designed by Robert Adam...take a walk in How Stean Gorge, also popularly known as Yorkshire's 'Little Switzerland'...visit Malham Cove, one of Britain's most impressive natural features...shop for bargains at the Tuesday market in Settle...walk to Hardraw Force... enjoy the rugged beauty of Swaledale and the prettier, and much busier, Wharfedale...and at the heart of the Dales admire or, if you're feeling fit, climb its highest peaks – Ingleborough, Whernside, Pen-y-ghent and Buckden Pike – or explore its caverns, potholes, and attractive villages and towns.

1 **Fountains Abbey**
The graceful stone arches of Fountains Abbey, the largest monastic ruin in Britain, which was founded by Cistercian monks in 1132.

2 **Pennine Way**
Britain's first long-distance footpath enters the Yorkshire Dales near Keighley and leaves past the Tan Hill Inn, covering 60 miles (97km).

3 **Cycling in the Dales**
The quiet back roads offer cyclists a superb way to explore the lush green pastures of the Dales.

4 **Hardraw Force**
Tumbling and splashing in a single, impressive drop over a limestone crag, this spectacular waterfall is situated behind the Green Dragon Inn.

5 **Limestone pavement**
The strange limestone landscape at Malham is riddled with natural cracks and fissures, where many unusual plants thrive in the dry, stony conditions.

6 Back o' th' Hill Farm
A colourful floral display welcomes visitors to the Buffers Coffee Shop, part of a working dairy farm near Bolton Abbey.

7 Ribblehead Viaduct
The 24 massive stone arches of the Ribblehead Viaduct carry the scenic Settle–Carlisle Railway line across the valley floor.

8 Swaledale
The lush green fields of Swaledale are divided by drystone walls. Many of the villages in this picturesque dale owe their origins to the lead-mining industry.

9 Ilkley Moor
Gritstone outcrops dominate the skyline all along Ilkley Moor. These attractive slabs, at the entrance to The Quarry and close to the famous Cow and Calf Rocks, are popular with climbers.

10 Pen-y-ghent
A fine drystone wall clings to the side of Pen-y-ghent, one of Yorkshire's famous Three Peaks. The hill is mainly carboniferous limestone topped with a cap of millstone grit.

9

10

Day One

For many people a weekend break or a long weekend is a popular way of spending their leisure time. These four pages offer a loosely planned itinerary designed to ensure that you see and enjoy the very best of the area. Options for wet weather and children are given where possible.

Friday Night

Stay at the Devonshire Arms at Bolton Abbey – it has been voted the best hotel in Yorkshire on several occasions. This is an expensive but worthwhile treat.

Saturday Morning

Visit the magnificent ruins of Bolton Priory, beautifully set amid woodland and pasture in a bend of the attractive River Wharfe. Near by are the notorious rapids known as the Strid.

Drive north on the B6160 to Grassington, and take the B6265 east towards Pateley Bridge, passing Stump Cross Caverns, with their truly dramatic subterranean formations – an excellent option on a wet day. In Pateley Bridge is the fine Nidderdale Museum, as well as craft and souvenir shops.

Saturday Lunch

A good choice for an enjoyable lunch is the Sportsman's Arms at Wath, located in Nidderdale, north of Pateley Bridge on the road towards Lofthouse. It is noted for its fish, and meals can be taken in the restaurant or the bar, with a stroll by the River Nidd to follow. Families might prefer Pateley Bridge, with its wide choice of pubs and cafés.

Saturday Afternoon

Continue northwards on the minor road towards Lofthouse, passing Gouthwaite Reservoir, and follow signs for the How Stean Gorge also known as Yorkshire's 'Little Switzerland'.

From Lofthouse head towards Masham, but just before the village of Healey take the Leyburn turning on your left, to bring you on to the A6108 at Jervaulx Abbey. Head in a northwest direction to reach Middleham, Yorkshire's smallest town, with tea shops, pubs, craft galleries and also a chance to visit the splendid ruins of Middleham's Norman castle.

Saturday Night

The Waterford House Hotel is small and reasonably priced, but is highly rated, especially for its fine, locally sourced food. If it is full, Middleham has a host of guesthouse and pub accommodation.

THE STRID

HORTON-IN-RIBBLESDALE

RICHMOND CASTLE

INGLEBOROUGH

Day Two

Our second day in the Dales takes in the very best of the area. A riverside walk, followed by a drive to a series of waterfalls, and one of the Dales' prettiest villages. Take lunch in a 'Herriot' hotel, see where they make Wensleydale cheese, and pass the dramatic Three Peaks.

Sunday Morning

Early risers can watch Middleham's racehorses training on the gallops above the town. After breakfast, drive from Middleham via Leyburn on the A684 up Wensleydale, with short diversions to Aysgarth to see its triple falls, and then to West Burton, a beautiful Dales village with one of the largest greens in the country. Continue on the A684, turning off into Askrigg, the heart of 'Herriot' country, where much of *All Creatures Great and Small* was filmed.

If the weather is wet, drive north from Leyburn on the A6108 to Richmond, with its castle and three contrasting museums. Return to the original route via the B6270 to Grinton and a minor road to Castle Bolton and then on to Aysgarth Falls.

Sunday Lunch

An ideal lunch spot is the King's Arms in Askrigg, with its old-fashioned back bar, filmed as the 'Drover's Arms' in *All Creatures Great and Small*, and a smart front bar serving a better-than-average choice of pub meals.

Sunday Afternoon

After lunch, head for Hawes, where the Wensleydale Creamery offers visitors a chance to watch Wensleydale cheese being made, it also has its own excellent museum and a fantastic cheese shop. If time allows, visit Dales Countryside Museum, which is in Hawes too, as well as a pottery and ropemaker.

Leave Hawes on the B6255 southwards for a lovely drive through a minor dale: Widdale. This is real Dales country and, full of walkers, the Pennine Way runs parallel to the road, and both the Dales Way and the Ribble Way cross it.

If time allows, pull over when you reach the unmistakable Ribblehead Viaduct, and hope your visit coincides with a train crossing on its way between Settle and Carlisle. Beyond the viaduct you can see Whernside, the highest of the Dales' Three Peaks at 2,414 feet (736m). In late April you might see the fit fell runners competing in the annual Three Peaks Challenge Race.

Turn left at the viaduct along the B6479 towards Horton in Ribblesdale, and you will pass between the other two peaks: Pen-y-ghent on your left, Ingleborough on your right. This road follows the River Ribble taking you all the way down into Settle, where you can enjoy afternoon tea at Ye Olde Naked Man Café before heading for home.

INFORMATION

Route facts

MINIMUM TIME The time
stated for completing each
route is the estimated
minimum time that a
reasonably fit family group
of walkers or cyclists would
take to complete the circuit.
This does not allow for rest
or refreshment stops.

OS MAP Each route is shown
on a map. However, some
detail is lost because of the
restrictions imposed by
scale, so for this reason, we
recommend that you use the
maps in conjunction with a
more detailed Ordnance
Survey map. The relevant
map for each walk or cycle
ride is listed.

START This indicates the
start location and parking
area. This is a six-figure
grid reference prefixed by
two letters showing which
62.5-mile (100km) square of
the National Grid it refers to.
You'll find more information
on grid references on most
Ordnance Survey maps.

CYCLE HIRE We list, within
reason, the nearest cycle
hire shop/centre.

❶ Here we highlight any
potential difficulties or
dangers along the cycle ride
or walk. If a particular route
is suitable for older, fitter
children we say so here.
Also, we give guidelines of
a route's suitability for
younger children, for
example the symbol 8+
indicates that the route
can probably be attempted
by children aged 8 years
and above.

Walks & Cycle Rides

Each walk and cycle ride has a panel giving information for
the walker and cyclist, including the distance, terrain, nature
of the paths, and where to park your car.

WALKING

All of the walks are suitable
for families, but less
experienced family groups,
especially those with younger
children, should try the
shorter walks. Route finding
is usually straightforward,
but the maps are for
guidance only and we
recommend that you always
take the relevant Ordnance
Survey map with you.

Risks

Although each walk has been
researched with a view to
minimising any risks, no walk
in the countryside can be
considered to be completely
free from risk. Walking in the
outdoors will always require a
degree of common sense and
judgement to ensure that it is
as safe as possible, especially
for young children.
• Be particularly careful on
cliff paths and in upland
terrain, where the
consequences of a slip
can be serious.
• Remember to check tidal
conditions before walking on
the seashore.
• Some sections of route are
by, or cross, busy roads.

Remember traffic is a danger
even on minor country lanes.
• Be careful around farmyard
machinery and livestock.
• Be prepared for the
consequences of changes in
the weather and check the
forecast before you set out.
• Ensure the whole family is
properly equipped, wearing
suitable clothing and a good
pair of boots or sturdy
walking shoes. Take
waterproof clothing with you
and a torch if you are walking
in the winter months.
• Remember the weather
can change quickly at any
time of the year, and in
moorland and heathland
areas, mist and fog can make
route-finding much harder. In
summer, take account of the
heat and sun by wearing a
hat, sunscreen and carrying
enough water.
• On walks away from
centres of population you
should carry a mobile phone,
whistle and, if possible, a
survival bag. If you do have
an accident requiring
emergency services, make
a note of your position as
accurately as possible and
dial 999 (112 on a mobile).

CYCLING

In devising the cycle rides in this guide, every effort has been made to use designated cycle paths, or to link them with quiet country lanes and waymarked byways and bridleways. In a few cases, some fairly busy B-roads have been used to join up with quieter routes.

Rules of the road

• Ride in single file on narrow and busy roads.
• Be alert, look and listen for traffic, especially on narrow lanes and blind bends and be extra careful when descending steep hills, as loose gravel or a poor road surface can lead to an accident.
• In wet weather make sure that you keep an appropriate distance between you and other riders.
• Make sure you indicate your intentions clearly.
• Brush up on *The Highway Code* before venturing out onto the road.

Off-road safety code of conduct

• Only ride where you know it is legal to do so. Cyclists are now allowed to cycle on public footpaths (yellow waymarkers). The only 'rights of way' open to cyclists are bridleways (blue markers) and unsurfaced tracks, known as byways, which are open to all traffic and waymarked in red.
• Canal tow paths: you need a permit to cycle on some stretches of tow path (www.waterscape.com). Remember that access paths can be steep and slippery so always push your bike under low bridges and by locks.
• Always yield to walkers and horses, giving adequate warning of your approach.
• Don't expect to cycle at high speeds.
• Keep to the main trail to avoid any unnecessary erosion to the area beside the trail and to prevent skidding, especially in wet weather conditions.
• Remember to follow the Country Code.

Preparing your bicycle
Check the wheels, tyres, brakes and cables. Lubricate hubs, pedals, gear mechanisms and cables. Make sure you have a pump, a bell, a rear rack to carry panniers and a set of lights.

Equipment

• A cycling helmet provides essential protection.
• Make sure you are visible to other road users, by wearing light-coloured or luminous clothing in daylight and sashes or reflective strips in failing light and darkness.
• Take extra clothes with you, depending on the season, and a wind/waterproof jacket.
• Carry a basic tool kit, a pump, a strong lock and a first aid kit.
• Always carry enough water for your outing.

Walk Map Legend

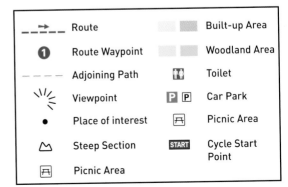

→ Route		Built-up Area
❶ Route Waypoint		Woodland Area
– – – Adjoining Path	🚻	Toilet
Viewpoint	P P	Car Park
• Place of interest	🛆	Picnic Area
⌂ Steep Section	START	Cycle Start Point
⛫ Picnic Area		

Ilkley
& the South

This region may not be the 'real' Yorkshire Dales, but it does mark their start. Here the industrial regions of Yorkshire give way first to the lonely moors around Haworth and Ilkley, then to the more open Dales landscape and the National Park to the north. It is an area that inspired the Brontës, that spawned the unofficial Yorkshire anthem ('On Ilkley Moor B'aht 'At') and that provided the dramatic locations and backdrops for *The Railway Children* and *Emmerdale*. Ilkley and Otley both stand in Wharfedale, while the River Aire runs by Haworth and Keighley on its journey eastwards from the Dales via Leeds to flow into the North Sea.

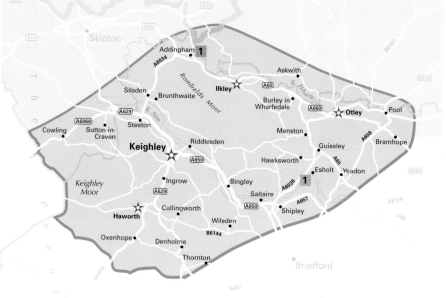

ILKLEY

TOP WITHINS

HOT SPOTS

Unmissable attractions

Explore Otley, a busy working town that *Emmerdale* fans will recognise...mingle with literary pilgrims hunting for the Brontë connection in Haworth...enjoy the wild moors and chic shops and restaurants of the elegant spa town of Ilkley.

1

1 Ilkley
Generations of walkers and climbers have left their mark on the rocks above the town of Ilkley.

2 Brontë Parsonage Museum, Haworth
The Parsonage was the home of the Brontë family. Its moorland setting gave the inspiration for their novel writing.

3 Otley
The Chevin looks down over the Lower Wharfedale town of Otley.

HAWORTH MAP REF SE0337

If the Reverend Patrick Brontë had not produced the literary offspring that he did, Haworth today would still be a very appealing but quiet town, noted for a steep cobbled street that leads up to its parish church, but no more. As it is, the Brontë Parsonage Museum, just beyond the church is flocked with visitors from all round the world, while beyond on the moorland, footpath signs in several languages direct thousands to the sites that inspired *Wuthering Heights*.

The one-time home of Patrick Brontë and his children (Emily, Charlotte, Anne and Branwell) is now a museum in which their lives and literary and artistic works can be studied in detail. Manuscripts and paintings attract as much attention as their living rooms, or the room in which Emily Brontë died at the age of only 30. It is an interesting place to visit for anyone who has ever read *Wuthering Heights* or *Jane Eyre*, but it is best to avoid Bank

Holidays and summer weekends when coach parties crowd the narrow corridors. There is more space to browse in the modern extension that houses most of the literary artefacts.

Outside the parsonage is the lovely parish church, where all the Brontës except Anne are buried in the crypt. Aside from its Brontë connections, it is a striking church with appealing stained-glass windows and statuary. Other Brontë links in Haworth – discounting such places as the Brontë Balti House – include the Black Bull Inn where Branwell drank, and the Old Apothecary where he bought his opium.

An earlier influence on the religious life of Haworth was John Wesley. He was a frequent visitor, and flocks of people would travel from as far away as Leeds to hear him preach. His sermons would start at dawn and last all day, his chapel overflowing. Wesley inspired William Grimshaw, who went on to spend the next 20 or so years as a Methodist minister in Haworth. By the time of his death in 1763 he was a household name.

Haworth itself is bulging with tea rooms and souvenir shops, and the tourist industry has meant that other visitor attractions have grown up, including the Brontë Weaving Shed, a reflection of the importance of wool in the industry in West Yorkshire. You can buy samples of the local Brontë tweed in the mill shop.

At the bottom of the very steep Main Street is Haworth's railway station on the Keighley and Worth Valley line, which is run by enthusiasts. Some of the line's old trains are on display here.

■ Visit

DARWIN GARDENS AND THE ORIGIN OF SPECIES

In 1859, Charles Darwin published *On the Origin of Species* and took refuge in the spa facilities at Ilkley as the repercussions began to materialise. Initially staying in Wells House, he was joined by his family and moved to North View House, now incorporated into the large building on the left at the top of Wells Road. To celebrate Ilkley's connections with the pioneering evolutionist, the former pleasure gardens across the road have been transformed into a Millennium Green known as Darwin Gardens with a maze, several monuments and rejuvenated paths and woodland.

ILKLEY MAP REF SE1147

Ilkley is quite a 'posh' place, as former spa towns tend to be. Antiques shops rub shoulders with expensive dress shops, which attract customers from all over the country, and in The Box Tree it has one of the best restaurants in the north of England.

It is also well situated, in the heart of the Yorkshire Dales to the north, easy access to Harrogate to the northeast and Leeds to the southeast. The River Wharfe runs through the town, and above it stands Ilkley Moor itself, where the original spa was located. This is at the White Wells, cottages built in 1756 by the landowner, Squire Middleton. These surrounded the spa and provided plunge baths for visitors, which were open-air but were later enclosed. Ilkley's growth began with the discovery of these mineral springs, whose particularly cold nature was believed to enhance their curative effects. Today the cottages contain a small museum, with displays about the Victorian spas as well as local wildlife and walks. Opening hours are limited, though – check to see if the flag is flying before venturing up the hill.

As the railway reached Ilkley in 1865, it brought regular visitors to such an extent that by the end of the century there were no less than 15 springs open to the public. The railways also brought wealth to the town with the arrival of industrialists from Bradford and Leeds, keen to find somewhere more pleasant to live. As a result, Ilkley now boasts some handsome Victorian architecture, with arcades of shops as well as more modern shopping precincts.

■ Visit

THE OXENHOPE STRAW RACE

One Sunday in each July, the village of Oxenhope near Haworth is transformed by this event, which goes back all the way to 1975. Rival teams compete to carry a bale of straw around the village, visiting – and drinking in – as many pubs as feasibly possible on the way. The race, which has a serious purpose in raising money for local hospitals, took off in a big way and now several hundred people take part (many in fancy dress) and several thousand watch them. There are various other activities over the whole weekend.

On Ilkley Moor, near the White Wells, are the dramatic Cow and Calf Rocks, and even if you prefer not to venture on to the moor itself, you should try to see these striking features. Local climbers practise on their sheer surfaces.

In the centre of town is the parish church of All Saints, well worth a visit for its Saxon crosses, two Roman altars and fine stained glass, some designed by the William Morris Gallery. A Burne-Jones window can be seen in the 1879 St Margaret's Church in Queens Road. In the gardens opposite is the Panorama Stone, the most accessible of the several prehistoric carved rocks in and around Ilkley town.

Next door to All Saints Church is the Manor House Museum. This is believed to stand on the site of the Roman fort of Olicana, which was built in AD 79, though many current theories dispute this. The museum has a small but interesting collection, and a gallery where modern exhibitions are displayed.

From Addingham to Ilkley

This walk takes you from the extended village of Addingham, through rolling country and along a stretch of the lovely River Wharfe to the spa town of Ilkley.

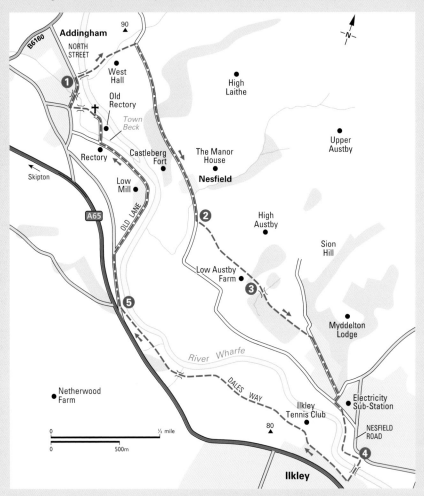

Route Directions

1 Walk 50yds (46m) up the road, and take stone steps down to the right, (signed 'Dales Way'). Bear immediately right again, and cross the River Wharfe on a suspension bridge. Follow a metalled path along a field edge. Turn over a stream at the end and follow a farm track left to emerge on the bend of a minor road. Go right here; after about 0.5 mile (800m) of road walking reach the community of Nesfield.

2 About 100yds (91m) beyond the last house, and immediately after the road crosses a stream, bear left up a stony track (signed 'High Austby'). Immediately take a stile between two gates. Cross to the gate in the far-right corner. Through it, there is no obvious path, but follow the boundary on your right, heading towards Low Austby Farm. Approaching the buildings, waymarks indicate the path dog-legging left and right outside the boundary wall, passing beneath a gnarled oak towards a wood.

3 Cross a footbridge over a stream; beyond a stile enter woodland. Follow a path downhill, leaving the wood by a step stile. Bear right across the slope of a field to a stile at the far end, to enter more woodland. Follow an obvious path through the trees, before reaching a road via a wall stile. Go right, downhill, to a road junction. Go right again, crossing Nesfield Road, and take a path to the left of an

electricity sub-station. After a few minutes of riverside walking reach Ilkley's old stone bridge.

4 Cross the bridge. This is your opportunity to explore the spa town of Ilkley. Otherwise turn right, immediately after the bridge, on to a riverside path (from here back to Addingham you are following the well-signed Dales Way). At its end, keep ahead along a drive to Ilkley Tennis Club. Beside the clubhouse, bear off left through a kissing gate and follow an obvious path across a succession of pastures, to the River Wharfe. Cross a stream on a footbridge, and enter woodland. Cross another stream to meet a stony path. Go right, downhill back to the river. Through another kissing gate, walk the length of a riverside meadow before joining the old A65.

5 Follow the road right by the riverside. After 0.5 mile (800m) of road walking, go right, just before terraced houses, on to Old Lane. Carry on between the houses at its end – Low Mill Village – to locate a riverside path at the far side. Once you have passed the Rectory on the left, and the grounds of the Old

Route facts

DISTANCE/TIME 5.5 miles (8.8km) 2h30

MAP OS Explorer 297 Lower Wharfedale

START Lay-by at eastern end of Addingham, on bend where North Street becomes Bark Lane by information panel, grid ref: SE 084498

TRACKS Riverside path and field paths, some road walking, 7 stiles

GETTING TO THE START Addingham is between Bolton Abbey and Ilkley. From the north, turn left along the road by the village's first houses. The lay-by is on the left, near the apex of a right-hand bend. From the south, leave the A65 road at the signpost for Addingham, then take two right-hand forks to reach the same bend.

THE PUB The Fleece Inn, Addingham. Tel: 01943 830491

❶ Short section by exposed riverbank just before Ilkley

Rectory on your right, look for a gate on the right. Take steps and follow the path to a tiny arched bridge over Town Beck. Swing left across a pasture, in front of the church. Cross a drive to an arched bridge, walking out between old stone cottages onto North Street in Addingham.

From Esholt to the Five Rise Locks

This cycle ride visits a few of the wonders of the Industrial Revolution, including Saltaire, the model village built by wealthy Bradford mill owner Titus Salt, and the Bingley Five Rise Locks. Saltaire was the result of Titus Salt's dismay at the overcrowded and unhygienic streets where many mill workers lived. He employed the best architects to design the village, covering an area of 25 acres (10ha), of more than 800 beautifully constructed houses for his workers.

Route Directions

1 Turn left out of the car park on to the road (with care) and descend to the village. The Woolpack, post office and row of cottages, as featured for many years on the TV soap *Emmerdale*, are on the left. Continue ahead down the lane, pass the Esholt Sports Club and a campsite. The terrace of Bunker Hill, right, was *Emmerdale's* Demdyke Row. Over a stone bridge and past a driving range the lane draws alongside the River Aire and then climbs right to meet the A6038 opposite the Shoulder of Mutton pub. It would probably be best to dismount here.

2 Turn left, following the footpath, then left again down Buck Lane. Soon take the

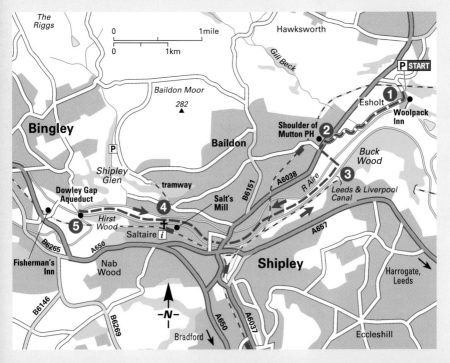

right fork, a mud and stone track descending to the River Aire. A steel bridge (1889) takes you to the far bank, where the track climbs to reach the Leeds–Liverpool Canal at Buck Wood.

3 Turn right along the tow path here. After about 100yds (91m) you'll come across a bench, which some kind soul has sited right next to bushes that in late August are endowed with the most luscious blackberries. The tow path is firm and wide at first, but beyond bridge 209a, carrying the railway to Baildon, it narrows considerably. If there are a lot of walkers about it would be best to follow the adjacent tarred lane and rejoin the tow path beyond the next bridge (209). Note: whichever route you choose, you will be crossing traffic at the second bridge. At this point the canal is cutting through the more industrial outskirts of Shipley, but soon things improve.

Some smart mill buildings and a tower appear. You're entering the model mill town of Saltaire. Spend some time here; it's a fascinating place.

4 The tow path continues along a very pleasing tree-lined section of the canal. Peeping through boughs on the left you'll see Titus Salt's church. At Hirst Wood just beyond Saltaire, the River Aire and canal draw closer together and the tow path continues on a narrow strip of land between the two.

5 The canal finally crosses the river along the Dowley Gap Aqueduct. If you want refreshments you can stop at The Fisherman's Inn, located a little further on down the canal. Afterwards retrace your route back along the canal to Esholt.

Route facts

DISTANCE/TIME 7 miles (11.3km) 1h45

MAP OS Explorer 288 Bradford and Huddersfield

START Esholt; grid ref: SE 182404

TRACKS All quiet country lanes and tow path

GETTING TO THE START
Esholt lies on the north bank of the River Aire to the north east of Bradford. Follow the A650 trunk road to Shipley, then the A6038 through Baildon, before turning right for Esholt. The car park is on the hill, just to the north of the town and near the railway viaduct.

CYCLE HIRE None locally

THE PUB The Fisherman's Inn, Bingley.
Tel: 01274 561697

❶ Busy road (A6038) at point 2; a steepish descent along the Buck Lane track to the river (Point 2).
Take care along the canal tow path.

■ Activity

KEIGHLEY'S WILDLIFE

Despite its origins in the industrial revolution, there is still a surprising amount of wildlife to be seen in Keighley. Bradford City Council and British Waterways have teamed up to devise a 3.5-mile (5.5km) walk which incorporates a stretch of the Leeds–Liverpool Canal tow path at Stockbridge Wharf, and the industrial heartland of the town, where visitors are reminded that they are still in Airedale by the presence of rabbits, foxes and the occasional badger. Details of the walk can be obtained from the Haworth Tourist Information Centre, as Keighley does not have a Centre of its own.

KEIGHLEY MAP REF SE0541

Although only about 3 miles (4.8km) north of Haworth off the A629, Keighley is a world away for the average visitor. Brontë pilgrims from America and Asia may flock to Haworth Parsonage – the home of the close-knit Brontë family, now a museum with displays of personal memorabilia – but few have probably even heard of this northern mill town, which, nevertheless, has plenty to offer visitors to the town.

Shoppers should note that, as well as the large modern Airedale Shopping Centre with its good selection of major department stores, Keighley has several of the north's traditional mill shops, through which factories would at one time sell their own goods to workers at reduced prices. These are now more commercial operations and sell a wide variety of goods, especially footwear, clothing, bedding and woollens.

Haworth and Keighley are linked by the Keighley and Worth Valley Railway, a 5-mile (8km) stretch of branch line, run by enthusiasts, which links with the Leeds–Settle–Carlisle main line at Keighley Station: platforms 1 and 2 are the main line, 3 and 4 the Keighley and Worth Valley Railway. The line was built to serve the valley's mills, and runs through the heart of Brontë country. At the station the concourse and booking hall have been beautifully restored to their late 19th-century splendour, complete with a glass canopy, and there is also a locomotive turntable on display, but the main attractions require a trip on the train. The first stop down the line is Ingrow West; here you will find the Museum of Rail Travel, where you can watch the restoration work taking place, and Ingrow Loco, a collection of steam locomotives centred around 'Bahamas', a Jubilee class engine rescued by enthusiasts in 1967.

The next stop is the gas-lit Damens Station, the smallest fully operational station in Britain, but a request stop only. Oakworth Station has also been restored in Edwardian fashion, complete with old tin advertisement signs and gas lamps. It may look familiar to anyone who has seen the film, *The Railway Children*. Haworth Station is next, and finally Oxenhope, where the main Railway Museum is situated and where there is also a buffet restaurant. The museum has a large collection of trains and carriages, including royal carriages and the train used in *The Railway Children*. There are also two tunnels along the line, and a good day out can be had by travelling the full length of it, stopping off at each station on the way. A journey along the line without stopping takes 25 minutes. The railway organises a varied programme of events for families and enthusiasts alike.

The first stop in Keighley should be the excellent Cliffe Castle Museum, a 19th-century mansion northwest of the town on the A629 road. The museum specialises in the geology and natural history of the region and has hands-on exhibits as well as touring exhibitions. One popular feature is a model of a giant newt, which used to live in the area. There are also Victorian toys, local historical items and a working beehive, the bees coming in and out through a tube, which leads to a hole in the wall.

The National Trust's East Riddlesden Hall, is situated 1 mile (1.6km) northeast of the town on the Bradford Road. This 17th-century Yorkshire manor house is set in 12 acres (4.9ha) with gardens and a medieval tithe barn housing a fine collection of agricultural implements. Inside the hall are mullioned windows, panelled rooms and good collections of furniture, pewter, embroidery and kitchen utensils, as well as the original kitchen and plenty of ghost stories from the helpful attendants.

OTLEY MAP REF SE2045

When the television series *Emmerdale* wanted a town that could give them a bustling livestock market for filming, they chose Otley in Lower Wharfedale. The town has had a market since Saxon times, and the first market charter was granted in 1222. There are cattle

■ Visit

EMMERDALE

The TV soap set in the Dales draws on a variety of local places for its inspiration. Otley becomes Hotten, with its market, and the opening titles flash through a mix of mostly landscapes in Wharfedale. Although originally made in Arncliffe in Littondale, until a few years ago the exterior shots for *Emmerdale* were filmed on location in the village of Esholt, between Leeds and Bradford. Now there is a purpose-built set in the grounds of Harewood House. This isn't open to the public, but Esholt is a worthy trip for fans.

markets on Monday and Friday, with general street markets on Tuesday, Friday and Saturday. Otley also has one of the oldest agricultural shows in the country, dating back to 1796. At first just a cattle show, today it is a highlight of the Otley calendar and includes rare breeds and the splendid shire horses.

Otley's parish church of All Saints has some Anglian crosses which date from AD 750, an early 14th-century tower, a Norman doorway and some lovely Victorian stained-glass windows, though the town's main attraction is simply itself. It is a busy working town, but with attractive 17th- and 18th-century buildings and streets with ancient names, such as Kirkgate, Bondgate and Boroughgate.

Thomas Chippendale, 1718–79, one of the world's most celebrated cabinet makers and designers, was born in Otley, where his family were joiners and where he served his own apprenticeship, probably at a shop in Boroughgate.

■ **TOURIST INFORMATION CENTRES**

Haworth
Main Street.
Tel: 01535 642329

Ilkley
Station Road.
Tel: 01943 602319

Otley
Nelson Street.
Tel: 01943 462485

■ **PLACES OF INTEREST**

Brontë Parsonage Museum
Church Street,
Haworth.
Tel: 01535 642323;
www.bronte.org.uk

Cliffe Castle Museum and Gallery
Spring Gardens Lane,
Keighley.
Tel: 01535 618231. Free.

East Riddlesden Hall
Bradford Road, Keighley.
Tel: 01535 607075
Manor house and tithe barn.

Keighley and Worth Valley Railway
Haworth.
Tel: 01535 647777 (timetable)
or 01535 645214 (enquiries);
www.kwvr.co.uk
Stations at Keighley,
Haworth, Oxenhope,
and Ingrow West.

Manor House Gallery and Museum
Castle Yard, Church Street,
Ilkley.
Tel: 01943 600066

Museum of Rail Travel and Ingrow Loco
Ingrow Railway Centre,
Keighley.
Tel: 01535 680425

White Wells Spa Cottage
Access on foot only from
Wells Road, Ilkley.
Tel: 01943 608035
Museum within the original
spa, stone plunge pool and
displays on Victorian ailments
and cures. Café.

■ **FOR CHILDREN**

Ilkley Toy Museum
Whitton Croft Road, Ilkley.
Tel: 01943 603855;
www.ilkleytoymuseum.co.uk
One of the finest private
collections of toys in the
North. Includes teddy bears
from before the First World
War and a 1930s dolls house.

Ilkley Lido
Denton Road, Ilkley.
Tel: 01943 600453
Dating from the 1930s, this
art deco open-air pool enjoys
views of the surrounding
moors and there's a heated
indoor pool next door.

■ **SHOPPING**

Ilkley
The main shopping areas are:
Brook Street, The Grove,
Victorian Arcade. Around the
main car park there are
shops on the Grove
Promenade and in a small

shopping centre. Specialist
shops include delicatessens,
books, fashion and antiques.

Keighley
The Airedale Centre is a large
shopping complex with many
major department stores.
Indoor market. Factory shop
in Lawkholme Lane.

Otley
Open-air market, Tue, Fri
& Sat.

LOCAL SPECIALITIES
Mill Shops
Ponden Mill, Colne Rd,
Stanbury. Tel: 01535 643500
The original mill bearing the
High Street brand is a large
18th-century textile mill, with
crafts, gifts, linen and
clothing.
Brontë Weaving Shed,
North Street, Haworth.
Tel: 01535 646217
Clothing and gifts.

■ **PERFORMING ARTS**

Ilkley Playhouse
Weston Road, Ilkley.
Tel: 01943 609539

Keighley Playhouse
Devonshire Street,
Keighley.
Tel: 01535 604764

King's Hall Complex
Station Road, Ilkley.
Tel: 01274 431576

Victoria Hall
Victoria Park, Hard Ings
Road, Keighley.
Tel: 01535 681763

■OUTDOOR ACTIVITIES & SPORTS

ANGLING

Fly

Ilkley: fishing on sections of the River Wharfe. Daily or weekly permits available from Ilkley TIC.
Tel: 01943 602319

Coarse

Keighley: Leeds–Liverpool Canal and along the River Aire. Permits are available from K L Tackle, 127 North Street, Keighley.
Tel: 01535 667574

CLIMBING

Ilkley

The Cow and Calf Rocks, situated on the edge of Ilkley Moor, are popular with local climbers. Permission is not needed.

COUNTRY PARKS, WOODS & NATURE RESERVES

Chevin Forest Park, Otley. Middleton Woods, near Ilkley.

HORSE-RIDING

Keighley

Truewell Hall Riding Centre, Holme House Lane, Goose Eye. Tel: 01535 603292
www.truewellequestrian.com

LONG-DISTANCE FOOTPATHS & TRAILS

The Dales Way

This 81-mile (130km) national trail follows, where possible, riverside paths from Ilkley to Bowness-on-Windermere. The Dales Way links the Yorkshire Dales National Park with the Lake District National Park.

The Ebor Way

A gentle 70 miles (112km) from Ilkley to Helmsley, this walk connects the Dales Way and the Cleveland Way, traversing most of Lower Wharfedale on the way.

The Worth Way

An 11-mile (17.5km) circular walk from Keighley up the Worth Valley.

The Brontë Way

This 43-mile (69km) walk connects Brontë-related sites from Birstall, near Bradford in the south, to Padiham in Lancashire, passing the Brontë birthplace at Thornton, and Haworth.

ORIENTEERING

Ilkley

There are permanent orienteering courses on Ilkley Moor and in Middleton Woods. For further information contact Ilkley Tourist Information Centre, Station Road.
Tel: 01943 602319

RUGBY

Keighley

Keighley Cougars Rugby League Football Club, Cougar Park, Royd Ings Avenue.
Tel: 01535 606044;
www.keighleycougars.info

Otley

Otley Rugby Union Football Club; Cross Green.
Tel: 01943 461180;
www.otleyrugby.co.uk

WATERSPORTS

Cowling

High Adventure, 233 Keighley Road. Tel: 01535 630044;
www.highadventureoec.co.uk
Watersports, climbing and adventure activity courses.

■ EVENTS & CUSTOMS

Haworth

Oxenhope Straw Race, Jul.

Ilkley

Ilkley Carnival, May Day Bank Holiday.
Literature Festival, once or twice a year.
Tel: 01943 601210
Wharfedale Festival of Performong Arts, week-long event, starts two weeks before Spring Bank Holiday.

Otley

Otley Show, Saturday before Spring Bank Holiday.
Otley Carnival, late Jun.
Christmas Victorian Fair, Dec.

Tea Rooms

Bettys Café Tea Rooms
32 The Grove, Ilkley LS29 9EE. Tel: 01943 608029; www.bettys.co.uk
The home of arch gentility on The Grove in Ilkley. Such is the reputation of this fine traditional tea room that you may find yourself queuing for a table on some busy days. But inside, you'll find that the cakes are truly magnificent, the tea, coffee and hot chocolate impeccable, and the decor as well mannered as you could ever imagine.

No.10 The Coffee House
10 Main Street, Haworth BD22 8DA. Tel: 01535 644694
Escape from the bustle of Haworth's Main Street to quiet rooms, where freshly brewed Fairtrade tea and coffee is served with a range of delicious home-baked cakes and Italian biscuits.

Cobbles and Clay
Main Street, Haworth BD22 8DA. Tel: 01535 644218
At the top of Haworth's cobbled Main Street, this colourful café combines with a pottery gift shop. You can sit outside in the cobbled hubub, retreat inside or go through to the balconied seating area at the rear with views across the Worth Valley.

Oxenhope Station Buffet
Oxenhope Station, Oxenhope BD22 9LD
KWVR's railway buffet is exactly that, a buffet car parked by the platform at Oxenhope Station. It isn't a very sophisticated place to eat, but if you like trains it's a treat and parking is free.

Pubs

Dick Hudson's
Otley Road, High Eldwick, Bingley BD16 3BA Tel: 01274 552121
On the far side of Rombald's Moor from Ilkley town, this is a famous old inn serving a standard range of modern pub food favourites as well as a good selection of beer and wine. Some people just come for the view though, which spans West Yorkshire all the way to Emley Moor.

Fleece Inn
67 Main Street, Haworth BD22 8DA. Tel: 01535 642172
A real pub in a town that sometimes feels a little too Brontëfied. That said, you can believe that Branwell Brontë paced the stone flagged floors of the bar, although the pleasant split-level dining area is a later creation. The Taylor's ales are excellent and the pub food has some interesting twists.

The Hermit Inn
Moor Lane, Burley Woodhead, Ilkley LS29 7AS Tel: 01943 863204
The hermit in question lived in a moorland shack in the 19th century. Now the pub that took his name is a popular moorside haven for locals and walkers. The food is locally sourced where possible and bookings are recommended at weekends.

Old Silent Inn
Hob Lane, Stanbury, Haworth BD22 0HW Tel: 01535 647437; www.old-silent-inn.co.uk
In a dip in the moors beyond Haworth, the Old Silent is a characterful 17th-century watering hole and restaurant. The name derives from a legend of Bonnie Prince Charlie seeking refuge here and the silence of the locals when questioned about his whereabouts.

Black Bull
Market Place, Otley LS21 3AQ. Tel: 01943 462288
Tracing its origins to the 16th century, Cromwell's troops are believed to have stopped here for refreshments on their way to battle at Marston Moor in 1644. Modern visitors can enjoy the excellent food and award-winning beers.

MALHAM

Gateway to the Dales

Skipton is the main claimant to the title of 'Gateway to the Dales', and it is the principal town on the A65 that runs along the southern boundary of the National Park and links the M1 and the M6. In fact, the road bypasses most of the interesting small towns alongside it, such as Settle and Giggleswick, and has delightful views of the hills to the north and, for much of the way, valleys and green fields dropping away to the south. Skipton also gives easy access to the most popular place in the whole National Park – Malham – and the varied attractions of the Bolton Abbey Estate.

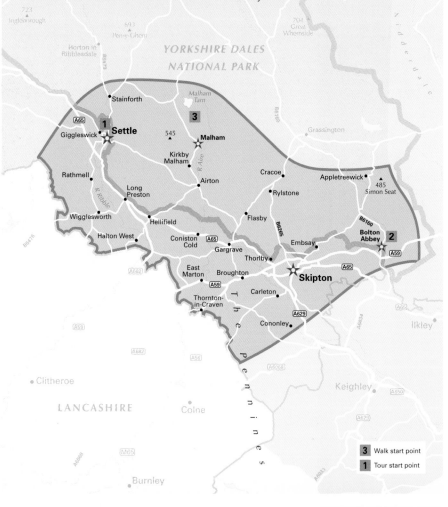

SICKDALE LANE NEAR SETTLE

GORDALE SCAR

LIMESTONE PAVEMENT, MALHAM COVE

Unmissable attractions

Visit Malham, a magnet for visitors, and walk the half-mile (800m) or so to Malham Cove, one of Britain's most impressive natural features...wander around Settle's Tuesday market where you'll find stalls crammed into Market Square and locals from the surrounding villages...walk around the magnificent Bolton Abbey Estate or visit Skipton Castle, one of the most complete medieval castles left in England.

1

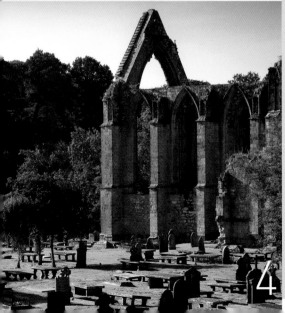

1 Whernside
At 2,415 feet (736m) high, Whernside is the highest of the Yorkshire Dales Three Peaks. Many walks around and up to Whernside's summit start near the Ribblehead Viaduct.

2 Gordale Scar
A footpath into this limestone gorge lies to the east of Malham. It's possible to climb up and then along the top of the Scar to enjoy spectacular views.

3 Skipton Castle
Standing at the head of the town's fine main street, Skipton Castle was restored by the remarkable Lady Anne Clifford after being damaged in 1648 during the Civil War.

4 Bolton Abbey
The substantial ruins of the 13th-century Augustinian priory, one of the showpieces of the Yorkshire Dales, lie in a peaceful setting by the banks of the lovely River Wharfe.

■ Visit

THE STRID

As the River Wharfe flows through the Bolton Abbey Estate, in one place it thunders through a narrow ravine just a few feet across – little more than a stride, or strid. If you feel a desire to jump across, bear in mind that several people have been killed as they slipped on the rocks and fell into the fast-flowing river, which is up to 30 feet (9m) deep in places. One of the leaflets handed to visitors asks them to 'remember that anything that goes into the Strid rarely surfaces for several days'. Be warned!

BOLTON ABBEY MAP REF SE0754

Bolton Abbey Estate is owned by the Duke of Devonshire and is an enjoyable amalgamation of recreational, historical and geographical, with guests at the Devonshire Arms enjoying the comforts of one of the best hotels in the country, and one of the region's best restaurants. For most people, though, Bolton Abbey is a day out in the car, within easy reach of the cities of Bradford and Leeds, with ample parking and plenty to see and do.

The first people to enjoy the site were the Augustinian monks who moved here from Embsay in 1154 to found a new priory. It was finished by the following century and now lies in evocative ruins in a meadow by the banks of the River Wharfe. The adjoining priory church of St Mary and St Cuthbert is far from being in ruins, though, and is one of the finest churches in the Dales. First built in 1220, it escaped the destruction of King Henry VIII's Dissolution of the Monasteries, only to fall one of many victims of dwindling congregations in the 1970s. Now restored, Bolton Abbey has breathtaking stained-glass windows and superb wall paintings.

If you drive along the B6160 to one of the car parks (day tickets allow you to move between several car parks so that you can explore the estate fully) you will pass under a narrow stone archway, part of an aqueduct that once carried water to the mill of which little now remains. There are shops on the estate selling Bolton Abbey-branded goods, as well as restaurants and a pub, many of them part of the village of Bolton Abbey, which grew up beside the priory.

There are many good walks to be had around the estate, including marked nature trails near the river and through Strid Wood, which is a Site of Special Scientific Interest. A leaflet showing the colour-coded walks is handed to visitors at the car park entrance. There are more than 60 different varieties of plants and about 40 species of birds nest there every year. Spring brings snowdrops and later whole rivers of bluebells, and in summer months the air is thick with dragonflies, butterflies and bees. Local nature groups post notices letting the visitors know what they are likely to see at the time of their visit.

A few miles north of Bolton Abbey on the B6160 are the imposing ruins of Barden Tower, built in 1485 and home to Henry, Lord Clifford, who was known as the Shepherd Lord because he was raised as a shepherd. The tower was later repaired by Lady Anne Clifford in the 17th century, but fell into disuse, although it remains an atmospheric site.

River and Woodland at Bolton Abbey

This walk takes you over moorland and alongside the Strid to the romantic Bolton Abbey. The route also passes through woodland where you'll find information boards explaining the birds and plants, including the sessile oak, which you will see on your way. Characteristic of the area, sessile oak is distinguished from the pedunculate oak by the fact that its acorns have no stalks.

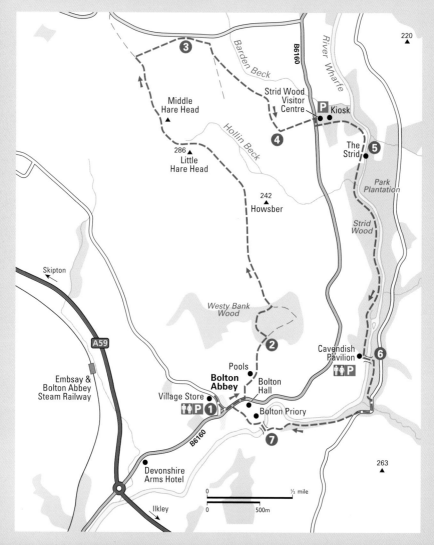

Route Directions

1 Leave the car park at its north end, by the Village Store. Turn right and walk to the B6160. Turn left and follow the road under an archway. Opposite the battlemented Bolton Hall, turn left on a signed track. At the top of the track, go through a gate on the right with a bridleway sign. Walk under a power line to a signpost. Go past two pools to a gate, then bear right to another gate into woodland.

2 Follow the rising track through the wood, with several signs, to another gate. Follow blue waymarks, most painted on rocks, across fields. At a crest bear left to a gate in a corner, then turn left along the wall. The path climbs more steeply onto Hare Head, which has wide views. Descend gently to a gate, and 20yds (18m) beyond, take a path downhill, trending right lower down, to a signpost.

3 Turn right on a path, parallel to the road, to another signpost 'FP to B6160'. Follow the track to a stile, then take the left fork, going roughly level across the moor, to a wall corner. Continue to the next wall,

then turn right along it, following an improving track to a signpost.

4 Turn left over a stile and follow the wall down to the road. Turn right a few paces then enter the car park. Pass beside the Strid Wood Visitor Centre and follow tracks, signed 'The Strid', down to reach the river close to its narrowest part at the Strid.

5 Follow wide tracks downstream until you reach an information board and gateway near the Cavendish Pavilion. Bear left by the café and cross the footbridge.

6 Immediately after the bridge turn right, signed 'Bolton Abbey'. The path briefly joins a vehicle track to cross a side-stream then bears right. When the path forks, take either branch (the higher has better views of the priory). Descend to a bridge beside stepping-stones near the priory.

7 Cross the bridge and walk straight on. Climb steps to a gateway – the Hole in the Wall. Go through to the road, left a few paces, then right to the car park at the start of the walk.

Route facts

DISTANCE/TIME 6.75 miles (10.9km) 2h30

MAP OS Explorer OL2 Yorkshire Dales – Southern & Western

START Main pay car park at Bolton Abbey, grid ref: SE 071539

TRACKS Field and moorland paths, then riverside paths, 3 stiles

GETTING TO THE START Bolton Abbey lies just to the north of the A59 between Skipton and Harrogate. Follow the B road past the Devonshire Arms. The main car park is on the left by the abbey and just before the village store.

THE PUB Devonshire Arms Hotel (Brasserie), Bolton Abbey. Tel: 01756 710441; www.thedevonshirearms. co.uk

❶ Navigation over the moors would be difficult in poor weather conditions. Dangerous river and currents around the Strid – read the warning notices.

MALHAM MAP REF SD9063

Malham is a magnet for visitors to the Dales. Malham Cove is one of Britain's most impressive natural features and consequently the area has become almost too popular for its own good. At busy times the National Park Centre car park overflows and the roadside verges disappear under the wheels of parked cars. The village streets give off a heady scent of cagoules and Kendal mint cake, and there are a number of cafés, pubs, outdoor shops and guesthouses to accommodate the crowds.

The half-mile (800m) walk to Malham Cove is signed from the village centre. The limestone rock face seems to tumble down the 250-foot (76m) cliffs, and extends for about 1,000 feet (305m). Try to picture the water that once flowed over the cliff face, helping create today what has been aptly described as a 'dry waterfall'. This natural amphitheatre was formed by movements of the earth's crust, and is simply the most visible part of the Craven Fault. It is a steep climb up man-made steps to the top, but your reward is an exhilarating view over the moors around Malham, north to Malham Tarn and over the limestone pavements that stretch away from beneath your feet. It is in these limestone pavements that some of the area's wide variety of unusual plants can be found.

Malham Tarn, to the north of the village, is in the care of the National Trust and the Field Studies Council. At approximately 150 acres (61ha), it can claim to be the highest natural lake in the Pennines. Malham Tarn is 1,229 feet (374m) above sea level, and both the tarn and the area around it have been declared a Site of Special Scientific Interest. A track leads down past Tarn House, where the Field Studies Council run regular courses on the natural history of the area. It is a particularly important area for plant life and as a breeding ground for many birds: a hide is open to the public to enable views of parts of the lake that can't be accessed on foot. Tarn House, a former shooting lodge, was also the home of Walter Morrison whose visitors at various times included Charles Darwin, John Ruskin and Charles Kingsley. It was while staying at Tarn House that Kingsley was inspired to write his children's classic, *The Water Babies*.

Malham's several other impressive natural attractions include Gordale Scar and Janet's Foss, one a limestone gorge, the other a magical waterfall, while the village of Kirkby Malham, a little way to the south, is also of interest. The church has many notable features, but one of the most significant is one of the three bells. It was cast in 1601 and weighs one and a quarter tons, making it the second largest bell in Britain.

SETTLE MAP REF SD8163

The day to visit Settle is Tuesday – market day – when stalls are crammed into Market Square and visitors jostle with locals from the surrounding farms and villages. Settle is quite a lot smaller than nearby Skipton, but it is a great place for shopping nevertheless, with some old-fashioned family-run stores adding to the appeal of its 18th- and 19th-century buildings.

The composer, Edward Elgar, had a very good friend in Settle, a Dr Buck. Elgar stayed with him often, in his house overlooking the Market Square, where a plaque commemorates the literary connection. Also overlooking the square is a two-storey row of shops known as the Shambles. In the 17th century this was an open market hall, which later became a butcher's shop. Arches and cottages were added in the 18th century, and then the second storey was built above the cottages in 1898. In front of the Shambles is a fountain pillar erected in 1863 to replace the former market cross, and in front of this is a café with one of the most unusual names you will ever come across: Ye Olde Naked Man Café. It kept the name of an inn, previously on this site, which called itself the Naked Man as a satire on the over-elaborate dressing habits of the time. Take a look behind Ye Olde Naked Man and you will see Bishopdale Court, typical of the many old yards and alleyways hidden away in Settle's streets.

One of the important natives of Settle is Benjamin Waugh, who founded the National Society for the Prevention of Cruelty to Children (NSPCC). He was born in a saddler's shop in what is now Lloyds TSB Bank, off the Market Square. Perhaps Settle's most unusual building is Richard's Folly, on School Hill, close to the Market Square. The house was built in 1675 for a local tanner, Richard Preston. He called it Tanner Hall, but it earned its 'folly' nickname because it stood empty long after Richard's death. It has since been restored and a part houses a museum.

■ Visit

THE QUAKERS

Airton, near Malham, is one of the largest villages in the Dales without a pub. This is due to the influence of the Quakers, who were forbidden to consume alcohol, in the 16th and 17th centuries. Visitors will have to seek refreshment by visiting the Friends Meeting House instead. This was founded by William and Alice Ellis, whose own house can still be seen, with their initials above the door.

■ Visit

THE BRIDGES OF MALHAM

In their haste to see Malham Cove, many visitors overlook the two old bridges in the village. The New Bridge, as it is known, is also called the Monks' Bridge and was built in the 17th century, then widened in the 18th. It can be seen near the post office. Malham's older bridge dates from the 16th century and is of clapper design, with large slabs of limestone placed on stone supports in the stream. This is the Wash-Dub or Moon Bridge, named after Prior Moon, the last Prior of Bolton Abbey, who had a grange in Malham.

West of Settle you'll find the rather oddly named Giggleswick. The village is renowned for its public school founded in 1553, and a much quieter place than Settle for visitors to wander around. Russell Harty, broadcaster and author, once worked as a teacher at the school.

To the west of Giggleswick, on the A65, is the Yorkshire Dales Falconry and Conservation Centre, with a collection of birds of prey from around the world. The outdoor aviaries are built from local limestone and very attractive.

A Circuit taking in Malham Cove

The noble Malham Cove is the majestic highlight of this limestone Dales walk. As you begin the walk, the stream from Malham Tarn suddenly disappears in a tumble of rocks. This is the aptly named Water Sinks. The now-dry valley of Watlowes, just beyond Water Sinks, was formed by water action. It was this stream in fact that produced Malham Cove, and once fell over its spectacular cliff in a waterfall 230 feet (70m) high. It is 200 years since water reached the cove. Beyond Watlowes valley you reach a stretch of limestone pavement – not the biggest, but probably the best known example of this unusual phenomenon in the Dales. The limestone slabs are known as clints, while the gaps between them are grikes.

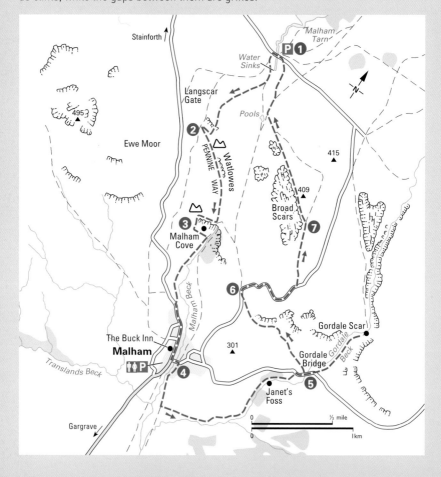

Route Directions

1 From the car parking space, walk through the gate, then turn left through the kissing gate at the Malham Cove sign. Keep left at the next signpost, following the Pennine Way down the dry valley until the path bends sharp right, overlooking another dry valley.

2 Turn left, cross a stile and descend steeply into the lower valley. Walk down the level valley to a stile at the end. Just beyond this is the limestone pavement at the top of Malham Cove. Turn right and walk along the pavement. Take great care here, both of the sheer drop down to your left and the gaps in the limestone pavement (known as grikes). Turn left to descend beside a stone wall; go through a gate, then descend more than 400 steps to the foot of the Cove.

3 At the bottom fork left to visit the very base of the cliff, then follow the obvious track beside the river. On reaching the road, turn left and follow it into the centre of Malham village. Turn left to cross the bridge.

4 Turn immediately right on a track past some houses, then continue along a gravelled path. Follow it left at a sign to Janet's Foss. Eventually the footpath enters woodland, then climbs beside a waterfall (Janet's Foss) to a kissing gate. Turn right along the road, towards Gordale Scar.

5 At Gordale Bridge (actually two bridges), go through a gate to the left. (To visit Gordale Scar, continue straight ahead here. Take a signed gate to the left and follow the path through a field into the gorge. Continue as far as the waterfall and then follow the same route back to the bridge.) On the main route, follow the signed public footpath uphill through three gates. Climb alongside a lane before emerging onto it.

6 Turn right and follow the lane uphill for 600yds (549m), to a ladder stile on the left. Follow a track to a footpath fingerpost.

7 Bear left and walk over a broad open moor before descending to some small pools. Turn right at a sign for Malham Tarn, go over a ladder stile, take the left-hand path and follow it back to the car park at the start of the walk..

Route facts

DISTANCE/TIME 6.25 miles (10.1km) 3h

MAP OS Explorer OL2 Yorkshire Dales – Southern & Western

START At Water Sinks, Malham Tarn, near gateway across road, grid ref: SD 894658

TRACKS Well-marked field and moorland paths, more than 400 steps in descent from Malham Cove, 5 stiles

GETTING TO THE START
Malham nestles at the head of the Aire Valley, 8 miles (12.9km) east of Settle. It is accessed by narrow lanes from Settle and from the A65 Leeds to Kendal road, between Gargrave and Hellifield. Drive through the village on the Malham Cove road, then turn right at the crossroads. The car park and start of the walk are on the left side of the road immediately south of Malham Tarn.

THE PUB The Buck Inn, Malham. Tel: 01729 830317; www.buckinnmalham.co.uk

❶ Some slippery sections on the limestone in the dry valley preceding Malham Cove. Steep drops from Cove's edge

Major Peaks and Minor Dales

This drive takes you through some of the minor but most beautiful dales such as Ribblesdale, Dentdale, Mallerstang, Deepdale and Kingsdale, and passes on the way the Three Peaks: Whernside, Ingleborough and Pen-y-ghent. You'll also be able to see the marginally smaller but equally dramatic hills of Wild Boar Fell and High Seat, on the northern boundary of the National Park.

Route Directions

The drive starts in Settle which has a helpful Tourist Information Centre and an enterprising museum, as well as busy pubs, cafés and the unusual buildings known as the Shambles.

1 From Settle take the B6480 north to its junction with the A65. Turn right on to the A65 travelling towards Kirkby Lonsdale. Turn right on to the B6255 to reach Ingleton, and its unique Waterfalls Walk. Ingleton is a small but friendly place with some steep streets, tourist shops and a fine parish church. Follow the signs 'Village Centre' and then 'Waterfalls Walk'.

2 At the start of the Waterfalls Walk, which is marked by a large sign, the road swings sharply left and then right again. Watch for the right turn along here signposted 'Dent'. Follow this road through Thornton in Lonsdale and turn sharp right by the church, still

following signs for Dent. This is a narrow, gated, but glorious road through Kingsdale, following Kingsdale Beck and then climb, with the summit of Whernside at 2,415 feet/736m on your right-hand side before descending steeply into Deepdale. Turn left at the next junction going towards Sedbergh. Continue left through the cobbled streets of Dent, which are delightful but not designed for drivers looking in vain for signposts, until you emerge on the other side. Continue towards Sedbergh, passing through the very green Dentdale and following the road round to the right. Bear left over the bridge at Millthrop and follow the road signed 'Town Centre'. Go straight on at the roundabout and turn right on to the main street in front of the Reading Room.

Sedbergh has a Wednesday market and there is also a large livestock market.

3 At the far end turn left, following the signs for Hawes, Kirkby Stephen and Brough. Follow the A683 alongside the River Rawthey and all the way out of the National Park with the dramatic Cautley Spout and the Howgill Fells to your left. From the moors the road descends towards Kirkby Stephen. Turn right on to the A685 into this unspoiled town between the Yorkshire Dales and the Lake District.

One attraction is its parish church of St Stephen, with 18th-century bread shelves and a 10th-century Norse stone cross.

4 In Kirkby Stephen turn right on to the B6259 for Nateby, staying on the road through Nateby and down through the valley of Mallerstang, with Wild Boar Fell on your right and Mallerstang Edge and High Seat, left. Wild Boar Fell rises to 2,323 feet/708m (higher than Pen-y-ghent at 2,274 feet/693m), and gets its name because the last wild boar in England was said to have been killed here. Its ruggedness remains an imposing sight.

5 At the T-junction by the Moorcock Inn, turn left on to the A684 towards Hawes but before you reach the centre of Hawes; turn right on to the B6255 towards Horton in Ribblesdale and Ingleton. This lovely winding road passes through Widdale and up and over Gayle Moor, bringing into view the magnificent sight of the spectacular Ribblehead Viaduct, carrying the Settle–Carlisle Railway line. The railway was built in the late 19th century, and is one of the most impressive feats of engineering. It is the most beautiful route in England, driving both under and over the Dales. Overlooking the railway line is Whernside, the largest of the Three Peaks, followed by Ingleborough and finally Pen-y-ghent. Though the smallest of the peaks, the brooding face of Pen-y-ghent has a special appeal.

6 Just before the viaduct, turn left on to the B6479 to pass through Horton in Ribblesdale, Stainforth and continue on to Settle. This road runs through

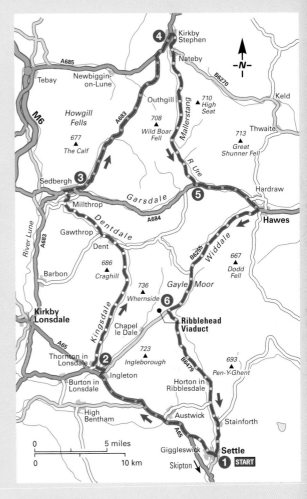

Ribblesdale with Ingleborough, right. Next, you'll see the unmistakable looming shape of Pen-y-ghent on your left. The road then runs along the banks of the River Ribble and back down into Settle.

SKIPTON MAP REF SD9851

Skipton buzzes with life, a busy, market filling its main street with stalls four days out of seven. It has modern shops, ancient inns, churches, a museum, restaurants and hotels, as well as a Norman Castle, over 900 years old but still in a superb state of preservation.

Skipton Castle is one of the most complete and well-preserved medieval castles in England. It was the birthplace of the indomitable Lady Anne Clifford and bears the Clifford family motto of *Desormais* (Henceforth) in large lettering above the splendid main entrance gate. The castle's huge appeal to visitors is indicated by the fact that there are tour sheets in several languages. Take one to find your own way around its warren of rooms. Some of the original Norman building remains, but most dates from the 13th century, later damaged during the Civil War but renovated by Lady Anne Clifford in the mid-17th century.

Beside the castle is the Holy Trinity Church, which dates mainly from the 14th and 15th centuries, although there was a church here the 12th century. It contains the tombs of many members of the Clifford family (though not Lady Anne), and a fine Tudor roof and screen.

Castle and church stand at the top of the High Street; half-way down is the Craven Museum, housed in Skipton's Town Hall. There is a small exhibition relating to one of Skipton's most famous sons, Thomas Spencer, of Marks and Spencer, who co-founded the company; other more conventional exhibits depict life ancient and modern in Skipton and the surrounding Craven area. One of the exhibits is a simple piece of cloth that was discovered in one of the Bronze Age graves near by. It is believed to be the oldest piece of cloth to be discovered in Britain. The museum is a good place to browse, wet or fine.

The oldest building in Skipton's High Street is the Red Lion Inn. It was built in either the late 14th or early 15th century and was once partly a farm. It is said to have been once owned by Richard III. Still visible in the forecourt of the inn is a bear-baiting stone.

But the town of Skipton, like Settle, is a place whose back streets need to be explored. There are also some pleasant walks to be enjoyed along the canal-side tow paths. Here the Leeds and Liverpool Canal passes through the town, joining on its way the Ellerbeck and Springs Canal, adding to the atmosphere that Skipton, for centuries, really has been the 'Gateway to the Dales'.

■ Activity

THE YORKSHIRE DALES CYCLE WAY

This almost circular route of 130 miles (209km) was devised by John Keavey of the Cyclists' Touring Club, at the request of the National Park Authority, with a view to giving cyclists an enjoyable and safe way of seeing the best that the Dales has to offer. The route begins and ends in Skipton, and is mostly on back roads that are waymarked with blue signs that carry a white cycle and a large direction arrow.

It is suggested that the average cyclist could tackle the route in six days, each day's stage being between 18 and 25 miles (28.9 and 40.2km). A folder containing full details and laminated maps for each section is available from National Park Centres and other outlets.

■ TOURIST INFORMATION CENTRES

Settle
Town Hall, Cheapside.
Tel: 01729 825192
Skipton
35 Coach Street.
Tel: 01756 792809

PARKING

Visitors are encouraged to use the pay-and-display car parks at the Yorkshire Dales National Park Centres to help relieve traffic congestion in the villages. Malham, in particular, gets very busy during peak holiday periods and at weekends.

■ PLACES OF INTEREST

Bolton Abbey Estate
Visitor centres and gift shops.
Tel: 01756 718009
Fee for the car parks.
Craven Museum and Gallery
Town Hall, High Street, Skipton.
Tel: 01756 706407
Embsay and Bolton Abbey Steam Railway
Skipton. Tel: 01756 710614 (general) or 01756 795189 (talking timetable).
Rides to Dales' villages and picnic spots.
Skipton Castle
Tel: 01756 792442
Very well-preserved medieval castle, birthplace of Lady Anne Clifford.

Yorkshire Dales Falconry and Conservation Centre
On the A65 near Giggleswick.
Tel: 01729 822832
Owls, hawks, falcons and eagles. Flying displays daily.
Yorkshire Dales National Park Centre
Malham. Tel: 01969 652380
Local literature, displays on the natural history, the local community and the work of conservation bodies. 24-hour information screen. Free.

■ FOR CHILDREN

Hesketh Farm Park
Near Bolton Abbey.
Tel: 01756 710444; www.heskethfarmpark.co.uk
Penned sheep, cows, pigs, goats and donkeys alongside an adventure play and indoor play area with a sandpit and a toy tractor zone.
Kirkby Field Visitor Farm Centre
Malham. Tel: 01729 830487
A chance for children to get close to animals including some rare breeds.

■ SHOPPING

Settle
Open-air market on Tue.
Skipton
Craven Court is a covered shopping centre in restored Victorian buildings. There are open-air markets on Mon, Wed, Fri and Sat.

■ LOCAL SPECIALITIES

Crafts
Watershed Mill Craft Centre, Watershed Mill, Langcliffe Road, Settle.
Tel: 01729 825539
Craft showroom, clothing, real ale, whisky and homeware.
Dorothy Ward, The Barn, Gargrave.
Tel: 01756 749275
Lamps, pottery, baskets, woollen goods.
Local Books & Maps
Archway Books, Commercial Court, Settle.
Tel: 01729 824009
Outdoor Equipment
Cave and Crag, Market Place, Settle.
Tel: 01729 823877
Cove Centre, Wallbridge Mill, Cove Road, Malham.
Tel: 01729 830432
Ultimate Outdoors, 1 Coach Street, Skipton.
Tel: 01756 794305
Paintings and Photographs of the Dales
Dales Pictures, Church Street, Settle.
Tel: 01729 823123
Walking Sticks
Many 'outdoor' shops sell traditional Dales carved walking sticks which are normally hand-carved from pieces of ash, blackthorn, hazel or holly.

■ OUTDOOR ACTIVITIES & SPORTS

ANGLING

Fly

Coniston Cold: A 24-acre (10ha) lake on Coniston Hall Estate. Tel: 01756 749551 or make arrangements through the hotel Tel: 01756 748080

Skipton: Fishing on the River Aire in and around Skipton. Contact Tourist Information Centre in Skipton. Tel: 01756 792809

BALLOON FLIGHTS

Skipton

Airborne Adventures, Old Burton Croft, Rylstone. Tel: 01756 730166; www.airborne.co.uk

BOAT HIRE

Skipton

For information about boat hire contact Skipton Tourist Information Centre. Tel: 01756 792809

BOAT TRIPS

Skipton

Various companies in the area operate boat trips along the Leeds and Liverpool Canal including Pennine Boat Trips of Skipton, Waterside Court, Coach Street. Tel: 01756 790829 Details of other operators are available from Skipton Tourist Information Centre. Tel: 01756 792809

CLIMBING & CAVING

There are innumerable opportunities for climbing and caving in the area. For guided instruction try Yorkshire Dales Guides, Langcliffe. Tel: 01729 824455; www.yorkshiredalesguides.co.uk

CYCLING

The Yorkshire Dales Cycle Way

This is a 130-mile (209.3km) circular route that starts and ends in Skipton.

CYCLE HIRE

Settle

Off the Rails, Station Yard. Tel: 01729 824419; www.offtherails.co.uk

Skipton

Dave Ferguson Cycles, 3 Albion Yard. Tel: 01756 795367

GUIDED WALKS

Several guided walks in the area are organised by the National Park Authority, Friends of Dalesrail and Dalesbus Ramblers. For more information contact the Tourist Information Centre in Settle.

Week-long or short break holidays walking in the Yorkshire Dales are organised by: HF Holidays Ltd, Catalyst House, 720 Centennial Court, Elstree, Herts. Tel: 0845 4707558

HORSE-RIDING

Yorkshire Dales Trekking Centre, Holme Farm, Malham. Tel: 01729 830352; www.ydtc.net

LONG-DISTANCE FOOTPATHS & TRAILS

The Pennine Way

The mother of all long-distance walks enters the area west of Skipton, before heading off over the fells from Malham.

The Six Dales Hike

A 42-mile (67.6km) walk through North Yorkshire from Settle to Skipton.

■ EVENTS & CUSTOMS

Malham

Malham Show, late Aug.

Settle

Maypole celebrations at Long Preston, Sat after May Day.

Skipton

Skipton Gala, early Jun. Game Fair, held at Broughton Hall, late Jun. Medieval Festival, early Dec.

Tea Rooms

Cavendish Pavilion
Bolton Abbey, Skipton BD23 6AN. Tel: 01756 710245; www.cavendishpavilion.co.uk
Bolton Abbey has a number of teashops but this one has the best setting, down by the river between the priory ruins and The Strid.

Wharfe View Tearooms
The Green, Burnsall, Skipton BD23 6BS
Tel: 01756 720237
Facing the Green, and beyond it the River Wharfe right in the centre of Burnsall, the Wharfe View is a favourite stopping place for walkers and motorists alike. Choose from a scrummy menu of cakes and sandwiches, then sit in the front garden and watch the world go by.

Beck Hall
Malham, Skipton, BD23 4DJ
Tel: 01729 830332; www.beckhallmalham.co.uk
Whether it's a for a sandwich, a light meal or a cream tea, Beck Hall is a great escape from Malham's busy village centre. Serving visitors since the 1930s it's the perfect place for contemplating your next walk or cycle ride, while you fill up on calorific but delicious Yorkshire curd tart or chocolate tiffin.

Ye Olde Naked Man
Market Place, Settle BD24 9ED. Tel: 01729 823230
This busy Market Place teashop and bakery takes its name from a peculiar relief carved above the doorway dated 1663. Inside you can fill up on tempting cakes or pastries or try a savoury pie. There is also a shop selling the café's produce and their delicious breads.

Pubs

The Angel
Hetton, Skipton BD23 6LT
Tel: 01765 730263
The reputation of this fine pub stretches beyond the fringes of the Yorkshire Dales. A string of awards, including from the AA, reflects its prominence as one of the best dining pubs in the North of England. The emphasis is modern British food, freshly cooked, using local beef, lamb, pork and cheese, and the fish is delivered daily from Fleetwood, Lancashire.

New Inn
Main Street, Appletreewick, Skipton BD23 6DA
Tel: 01756 720252
New Inn positively welcomes walkers, cyclists and visitors, proclaiming itself to be the first 'Mountainbike Livery' in the area. There's good food and decent beer on offer too, amid the photos and maps that adorn the walls inside.

Lister Arms
Malham, Skipton BD23 4DB
Tel: 01756 830330
An old coaching inn at the heart of Malham village, it is to its credit that it caters so well for the summer hordes while retaining a villagey feel inside. Diners will find an interesting mix of modern and traditional food, and there's always a children's menu. Beer lovers may be tempted by the dazzling array of Belgian beers as well as the reliable stock of British cask and bottled ales.

The Woolly Sheep Inn
38 Sheep Street, Skipton BD23 1HY
Tel: 01756 700966
At the foot of Skipton's main shopping street, the Woolly Sheep is a Taylor's pub, serving excellent beer and home-cooked food, which means the usual mix of steak, chicken, Cumberland sausage and scampi. Inside you'll find the interior is everything you would expect from a traditional pub in a market town, and it is this reliability that gives the Woolly Sheep the edge over the town's many other pubs.

Harrogate & Ripon

This is the 'civilised' corner of the Dales, where the landscape is pleasantly rolling – even flat in places – and will appeal to car drivers and those who like strolling round sights, rather than serious walkers who prefer to trek across the high hills of the wilder Dales. It contains one of Britain's most visited and most scenic attractions in Fountains Abbey, magnificent even in its ruined state, surrounded by the beautifully landscaped Studley Royal Gardens. There is the cathedral city of Ripon to explore, and refined Harrogate, not to mention Old Mother Shipton's Cave in Knaresborough.

FOUNTAINS ABBEY

PATELEY BRIDGE

NEAR PATELEY BRIDGE

HOT SPOTS

Unmissable attractions

Marvel at the strange natural sculptures at Brimham Rocks...choose between attractions such as Fountains Abbey – a World Heritage Site – and Newby Hall – award-winning gardens – which vie for attention around Ripon...explore Ripley, a charming estate village built around Ripley Castle, which contains the National Hyacinth Collection, as well as walled gardens, old hothouse buildings and a woodland walk...explore Ripon's magnificent cathedral, which houses a Saxon crypt dating from AD 672...take a shopping expedition to Harrogate and enjoy the many shops, theatres and colourful gardens...visit Knaresborough, one of the most picturesque market towns in the Dales with a fantastic castle to explore.

1 Brimham Rocks
This group of weathered rock formations has long been a popular playground and picnic place. Standing in high open moorland, the area is owned by the National Trust.

2 Knaresborough Castle
Knaresborough's Castle, once a significant Royalist stronghold was reduced to a dramatic shell by Parliamentarian forces after the Civil War.

3 Pateley Bridge
The bustling town of Pateley Bridge, at the heart of delightful Nidderdale, is a deservedly popular destination with visitors.

4 Fountains Abbey
Designated a World Heritage Site in 1987, exquisite Fountains Abbey is one of the largest monastic ruin in Europe.

5 Newby Hall and Gardens
The fine 18th-century mansion of Newby Hall was designed by Robert Adam and incorporates an elaborate tapestry room and two galleries of Roman sculpture.

6 Harrogate
The Stray, a wide open space of trees, lawns and flowers in Harrogate, sweeps majestically through the centre of town.

BRIMHAM ROCKS
MAP REF SE2165

Just off the B6265, 4 miles (6.4km) east of Pateley Bridge, these 50 acres (20ha) of fantastic natural rocks standing amid Nidderdale's moorlands should not be missed. Nowhere will you see a sight quite like them – blocks and boulders 20 feet (6m) and more in height, weathered simply by natural forces – wind, rain, frost and ice – into strange and surreal shapes. They have attracted tourists since the 18th century, and over the years some have acquired names, such as the Blacksmith and Anvil, the Indian Turban, the Sphinx, and the Dancing Bear, giving some idea of the shapes these rocks of dark millstone grit have been twisted into. So odd are these shapes that it is hard to believe they were not created by a team of talented sculptors. One in particular, known as the Idol, is enormous and seems to be improbably balanced on a rock scarcely the size of a dinner plate. There is also a Kissing Chair and, of course, the inevitable Lover's Leap.

■ Insight

BRIMHAM MOOR
The area of the rocks and surrounding moorland appears in the Domesday Book as Birnbeam, and at that time the land was, like much of the Dales, forested. The monks of Fountains Abbey cleared the trees from the landscape to enable them to farm it, thus also exposing the rocks to the elements, although the basic shapes were created about a million years ago during the ice age, the ice working on rocks that were first deposited some 200 million years ago.

There is a car park at the entrance of the site, and a choice of several walks through the area, which in all extends for 387 acres (157ha) around the rocks themselves. Some paths go off into the undergrowth, but an easier central path leads to Brimham House, converted into an information centre with refreshment facilities and a shop attached. A superb viewpoint indicates the sights for some distance all around.

FOUNTAINS ABBEY
MAP REF SE2768

To describe Fountains Abbey as a ruin does it a disservice, and even the term 'remains' does not prepare the visitor for the awesome and graceful sight of the best-preserved Cistercian abbey in Britain. It looks as if it may have been only a few years ago that the monks finally moved out. Fountains Abbey was justifiably designated a World Heritage Site in 1986, and is one of the largest monastic ruins in Europe.

Fountains Abbey was founded in 1132 by a group of monks who actually left a Benedictine abbey in York because the order was not strict enough for them. The buildings you see today were mostly constructed in the years from 1150 to 1250, though the North Tower, which looms up into the sky, is a 16th-century addition. This is called Huby's Tower, named for Marmaduke Huby, the abbot who had it built not long before the Dissolution of the Monasteries.

In medieval times Fountains Abbey was the richest abbey in Britain; it owned a great deal of the land in the Yorkshire Dales, and used it for grazing large herds of cattle and sheep. Visitors travelling around the Dales today will come across constant references to land that once belonged to the abbey, and buildings that were once its granges (outlying farms). Sheep-rearing and the resultant meat and cheese were a large source of revenue for the monks, and visitors can only try to imagine the wealth that would ensue if a single land owner or estate farmed the same area of land today.

A visitor centre was added in 1992 amid some controversy and fears that it would intrude on the beauty of the abbey itself, but hidden well away as it is, the centre caters well for the 300,000 people who visit the site each year. Its design ensures that while Huby's Tower can be seen from the centre, to give a sense of the abbey's presence, the centre can't be seen while walking around the abbey estate. The visitor centre incorporates an auditorium, a restaurant and kiosk and the largest National Trust shop in Britain. You can also see the recently beautifully restored monastic mill, and a handful of rooms in Fountains Hall, the 17th-century home of the subsequent owners of the abbey.

The adjoining grounds of Studley Royal were created in the 18th century and then merged with Fountains Abbey in 1768. They were the lifetime's work of John Aislabie, and then his son, William. John Aislabie inherited the Studley Royal estate in 1699 when he was Treasurer of the Exchequer, but involvement in the disastrous South Sea Bubble left him free to spend more time with his garden. The landscaping took 14 years, then another decade for the construction of the buildings. There are several paths around the gardens, through which the River Skell flows, and acquiring a map is probably a good idea as there is a great deal to see here including fine temples and water cascades. Nineteenth-century St Mary's Church, built by William Burges, is the focal point of the 400-acre (162ha) deer park, home to a good-sized herd of about 350 red, fallow as well as Manchurian sika deer.

■ Activity

ROLL OUT THE EGGS

Parents of young children might like to know that the Easter Monday egg-rolling tradition was revived at Fountains Abbey in the 1980s, at the suggestion of an estate worker who recalled the tradition from his own childhood. Hard-boiled eggs are thrown or rolled down a hill, a prize being given to the one that goes the furthest before disintegrating completely. In some areas, children would decorate their eggs and put them on display, before rolling them down the nearest slope and finally eating any eggs that remained edible.

■ Insight

THE SOUTH SEA BUBBLE

The South Sea Company, formed in 1711, monopolised trade in the South Seas and South America. The bubble 'burst' in 1720, and in the following year John Aislabie, Chancellor of the Exchequer, was sent to the Tower of London charged with fraud. He served a short sentence and was then dispatched back to the north of England, his career in ruins. He appears to have had some money left over, judging by the extent of the work done on Studley Royal, for which 100 men would be employed each year for the manual work alone.

The Harland Way

The Harland Way forms the basis of a delightful rural ride following in the tracks of the steam trains and visiting one of Yorkshire's most fascinating Norman castles at Spofforth. Lying among the peaceful pastures of the Crimple Valley, Spofforth is an idyllic backwater for a Sunday afternoon ride.

Route Directions

1 With your back to the car park entrance, turn right along the railway trackbed, highlighted by a Harland Way fingerpost. The old line has been exploded through the bedrock to reveal limestone crags, and is now hung with lovely woodland that offers plenty of welcome shade on hot sunny summer days.

2 Take the left fork at the road junction that used to be known as the Wetherby Triangle. You are soon joined from the right by another branch of the line and then together the routes head west towards Spofforth. Half-way along the track you have to dismount to get through a metal gateway and almost immediately again at another gate. The trackbed forges ahead through an avenue of beech, hawthorn, ash and rowan before coming out into the open. Now you'll see thickets of wild roses and bramble, with scabious and purple vetch among the numerous wild flowers of the verges. Here there are wide views across cornfields, and soon the tower of Spofforth church comes into view ahead of you.

3 The Harland Way ends beyond a gate just short of the village. Take a gravel path which veers right across a green on to East Park Road. This threads through some modern housing to come to the main road where you should turn right. If you have young children it might be better to dismount here to cross over the road, and use the pavements to get to The Castle Inn.

4 Just beyond the pub, where the road bends to the right, take the lane on the left, which heads for the castle. When you've explored the 14th- and 15th-century remains of Spofforth Castle retrace your route past the pub then turn right along Park Road. Beyond the

Route facts

DISTANCE/TIME 8 miles (12.9km) 2h

MAP OS Explorer 289 Leeds

START Sicklinghall Road, Wetherby, grid ref: SE 397483

TRACKS Well compacted gravel railway trackbed lanes and smooth bridleways

GETTING TO THE START From the A661 Wetherby to Harrogate road turn off on the westbound Sicklinghall road and then after just 300yds (274m) a blue cycleway sign points to the car park on the right.

CYCLE HIRE None locally

THE PUB The Castle Inn, Spofforth. Tel: 01937 590200

❶ A short section of main road through Spofforth

houses this becomes a stony bridleway, which rises gently across the fields.

5 Ignore all turn-offs until you come to Fox Heads Farm. Turn left along the track here, passing left of the farmhouse. The dirt and stone track descends to a bridge over a stream, then climbs again past an old quarry. Though there are a few climbs the track is still quite easy, being smooth-

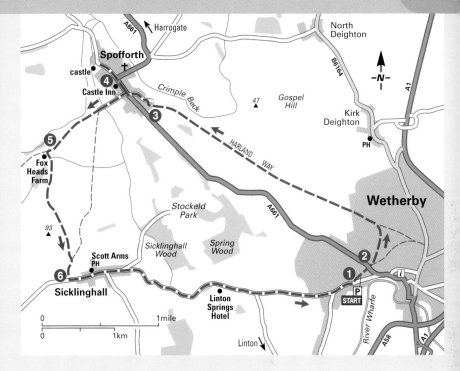

surfaced and reasonably well drained. Often it's lined with bramble, ferns and foxgloves, and the odd tree. Just beyond the summit of a hill the track bends to the right. After being joined from the right by a second farm track it comes to the road, just to the west of Sicklinghall village.

6 Turn left along the road into the village. On the right there's a pond with lilies and coots, then on the left there's another pub, the Scott Arms. The winding road makes a long but gradual descent towards Wetherby, passing the upmarket Linton Springs Hotel on your right. Beyond the hotel, ignore the right turn 'to Linton'. After passing through some housing in the Wetherby suburbs watch out for the blue cyclists' sign. This marks the access road back to the car park.

HARROGATE MAP REF SE3054

Although not within the Yorkshire Dales as such, Harrogate is by far the largest town on their fringes, and a magnet for anyone with serious shopping – or just window-shopping – to be done. It is an attractive and lively place with theatres, cinemas and good restaurants, and a plethora of new hotels and conference centres created by the busy hospitality industry. But Harrogate has not lost its charm, and the spa town that developed after the discovery of a spring in 1571 is still plainly visible.

An important feature of Harrogate is its lush greenery, especially the wide swathes of grass and flower beds,known as the Stray, that sweeps right through the town. These 200 acres (81ha) are protected under an ancient law, which ensures that residents and visitors alike are entitled to enjoy these recreational facilities. There are more pretty flowers as well as a boating pond, playground, crazy golf and plenty of other activities in the Valley Gardens, Harrogate's main park. Its entrance is close to the Royal Pump Room Museum.

Flower lovers will not want to miss a visit to the Royal Horticultural Society Garden at Harlow Carr on the outskirts of Harrogate off the B6162. This was the HQ of the Northern Horticultural Society (until its merger with RHS in 2001) and is set in 68 impressive acres (28ha), a lovely mix of the formal and informal, with a gardening museum, plant and gift shops, and places for refreshments. Several courses, demonstrations and practical workshops are held in the Study Centre, and there is even a branch of Bettys.

Harrogate's origins can be traced in the octagonal Royal Pump Room Museum, which was built in 1842 in order to enclose the old sulphur well on this site. In addition to serving up local history, the museum serves up cups of the pungent spa water that first made the town so famous. It claims to be the strongest sulphur water in Europe, so some visitors may prefer Perrier, or to refresh the palate with a visit to Bettys tea rooms, a real Yorkshire institution, which offers delicious cream cakes and Yorkshire Fat Rascals.

Not quite a Yorkshire institution is a visit to a Turkish baths, and perhaps it is just a coincidence that the entrance to the baths is just a short stroll down Cambridge Road from Bettys. Harrogate is one of the few places where you can enjoy a Turkish bath in all its original 19th-century splendour at the Turkish Baths and Health Spa in the Royal Baths Assembly Rooms. Its original Victorian exterior masks a beautifully renovated tiled interior, which includes a cold plunge bath, several hot rooms, a steam room, massage room and a relaxing rest room for when the ordeal is over. There are both male and female sessions, so check first if you are thinking of going.

You can glimpse a snapshot of Victorian life through the paintings of William Powell Frith. The son of a Harrogate hotelier, Frith specialised in narrative painting in a very traditional style. The municipal Mercer Art Gallery on Swan Road has many of his pieces among over 2,000 works from the 19th and 20th centuries.

1899

■ Visit

THE HOUSE IN THE ROCK
This folly was carved out of the rock face by a local weaver, and is still lived in as a private dwelling. It can be found up the steps by St Robert's Chapel, also carved out of the rock in 1408. The Chapel is off Abbey Road, beyond Low Bridge.

■ Visit

THE NEWGATE CONNECTION
As you approach the Garden Restaurant at Newby Hall, an old wooden door, hanging to the left of the entrance gates bears the inscription: 'Through these gates Jack Sheppard, highwayman, escaped from Newgate Prison, 30th August 1724'. The doors were brought to Newby in the 19th century when the Hall passed by marriage to the Vyner family from Lincolnshire. Several Vyner ancestors had been Lord Mayor of London.

KNARESBOROUGH

MAP REF SE3557

Knaresborough is considered to be one of the most picturesque market towns in the Dales, much of it perched on ridges of rock rising above the River Nidd, on which rowing boats are usually bobbing about. A viaduct crosses high above the river, while old houses peek through the trees on one side, looking across at the parkland and woods that conceal Mother Shipton's Cave on the opposite bank.

In the time of Mother Shipton, the Yorkshire prophetess, this land was a large hunting forest, and Knaresborough must have looked even more beautiful than it does now. Mother Shipton, said

to have been born in the cave in 1488, gained a reputation as a prophet. It is claimed that she foretold the attempted invasion and subsequent defeat of the Spanish Armada in 1588, and predicted the devastating Great Fire of London in 1666. You can visit the cave as part of a self-guided audio tour, along with the Petrifying Well – in which minerals in the water turn any object placed inside it to stone – and a small museum.

The town's official museum is up in the Old Courthouse in the grounds of Knaresborough Castle. It houses local items and a gallery devoted to the Civil War in Knaresborough, but is enjoyable not least because Knaresborough seems to have had more than its fair share of rather odd characters over the years, and their doings are well chronicled. In addition to Mother Shipton there was Robert Flower, who lived in a cave on the riverside and was known locally as St Robert because of his alleged powers as a miracle healer; Eugene Aram, a wicked schoolmaster who murdered a shoemaker in St Robert's cave and managed to escaped justice for 13 years; and John Metcalfe, who went blind at the age of six, but later went on to enjoy various careers including, quantity surveyor, road building pioneer, accomplished violinist and part-time smuggler!

These days, Knaresborough Castle is much reduced, but it has also seen its fair share of characters over the years. The murderers of Thomas a Becket sought refuge here for a time, and royal visitors included Edward III, King John and Richard II, who was imprisoned here in 1399. The dungeon remains just as it was. There are knowledgeable guides on hand to answer questions, and regular tours of the sallyport (a secret access to the moat). With a small park around the remains, this is a popular spot to sit and enjoy the lovely views over the river.

Not far away is the market place, where, as well as a bustling Wednesday market, you will find the oldest chemist's shop, or apothecary, in Britain, thought to have been established in the 13th century, but trading continuously since 1720. The market is first mentioned in 1206, but is known to have been held each and every Wednesday since 1310, the day fixed by Edward II's charter.

The Church of St John contains some Norman remains, and a Tudor font with a lockable cover to prevent witches stealing the holy water. By the church, a street named Water Bag Bank descends steeply to the river. The unusual name arose because the town's water supply was once brought up here on horseback in leather bags.

NEWBY HALL MAP REF SE3468

Newby Hall is rather hidden away in the countryside southeast of Ripon, but it's well worth seeking out even though it is inevitably busy on summer weekends and Bank Holidays. The 17th-century mansion, with interiors added by Robert Adam and which many believe to be one of the finest stately homes in England, is signposted off the Ripon–Boroughbridge road, the B6265, near Skelton.

Although there are no guided tours, estate staff are on hand in the rooms and corridors to answer any questions.

An informative booklet gives details of the many rooms that are on public view. The billiard room is particularly fine, and contains a splendid portrait of Frederick Grantham Vyner, an ancestor who was murdered by Greek bandits. There is a statue gallery, Chippendale furniture to admire, an overwhelming tapestry room, its walls covered in 18th-century French tapestries, and, by way of contrast, an collection in the chamber-pot room.

Outside the hall, you'll find that the award-winning gardens are extensive and will appeal as much to horticultural experts for their plantings as to those who can simply admire the beauty of their design. The credit for their design and development goes to the present owner's father, Major Edward Compton, who transformed the grounds from a nine-hole golf course into gardens that have been specifically created to offer something different in every season of the year. Leaflets suggest the best walks to appreciate the many seasonal highlights, another details the National Collection of *Cornus* (Dogwood), which is held here. The Woodland Discovery Walk is a stroll through an orchard, down to the River Ure, crossing a restored rustic bridge and back up to reach Newby Hall through Bragget Wood. The walk has been created with the help of Yorkshire Wildlife Trust, hence the wealth of good information in the booklet.

Children will enjoy the miniature railway which runs alongside the banks of the River Ure, and near by is an adventure garden with a timber fort, climbing frames, pedaloes, swing boats and an interactive water play area.

PATELEY BRIDGE
MAP REF SE1565

The main attraction at Pateley Bridge is the Nidderdale Museum, but the town is also a good base for visiting places of interest near by. Many of the buildings date from the 18th and 19th centuries, when the town flourished with thriving local industries and the vital arrival of the railway, though as it is built of gritstone it can appear to be a rather dour place in gloomy autumnal weather.

However, you'll find that there is nothing dour about the award-winning Nidderdale Museum, housed in the town's former workhouse. Founded in 1975, it grew from just a very small collection to one which today provides all the information you need about life in Nidderdale, from the spread of religion and the development of transport to collections of cameras and razors that have been owned by local people. Some of the most enjoyable exhibits are the reconstructed cobbler's shop, general store, milliner's shop, joiner's shop and solicitor's office. All contain fascinating memorabilia, and the whole museum is much loved and well looked after.

To the north of Pateley Bridge, near Lofthouse, is How Stean Gorge, also known as Yorkshire's 'Little Switzerland'. The ravine of up to 80-foot (24m) deep was hacked out in the ice age. Pathways lead by the fast-flowing river through ferns and by lush, dank undergrowth; there are bridges on different levels and fenced galleries on rocky ledges. There are also a few caves, the best known being Tom Taylor's Cave, with a 530-foot (162m) walk underground (take a torch).

To the west of Pateley Bridge, on the B6265, are the Stump Cross Caverns. Only discovered in the mid-19th century, the caves have given up fossil bones as much as 200,000 years old, many from the wild animals such as bison, reindeer and wolverines that once wandered the region. Visitors can also see the usual stalactites and stalagmites with appropriate names.

RIPLEY   MAP REF SE2860

Ripley is an estate village built around Ripley Castle, which has been home to the Ingilby family since the 1320s. Guided tours (taking about 75 minutes) are available, with the guides providing many colourful anecdotes about the castle's past owners and visitors. A superb plaster ceiling was put into the Tower Room with the specific intention of impressing James VI of Scotland as he passed through Ripley on his way to accede the throne as King James I of England. There are fine collections of weaponry and furniture, as well as secret hiding holes and passageways.

The gardens contain the National Hyacinth Collection, as well as walled gardens, old hothouse buildings and a walk through the wooded grounds to take in a hilltop gazebo. One of the herbaceous borders in the walled gardens is no less than 120 yards (110m) long, making not merely a splash of colour but a positive swimming pool.

Ripley village was largely built in the 1820s by Sir William Amcotts Ingilby, an affable eccentric who modelled it on an estate village he had seen in Alsace-Lorraine. The delightful result is the only place in Yorkshire which has a 'Hotel de Ville' rather than a Town Hall, and the cobbled Market Square with its stocks, the listed cottages, and the 15th-century church all make this an unusual and pleasurable place to visit.

RIPON MAP REF SE3171

In AD 672 St Wilfrid built a church on the site of what is now Ripon Cathedral, and the crypt of that church can still be visited, making it the oldest complete Saxon crypt in any English cathedral. The west front of this splendid cathedral dates from 1220, the east front from 1290, and inside there are 500-year-old woodcarvings, a 16th-century nave and some exceptional stained-glass work. All-in-all, a building not to be missed.

Close by, in St Mary's Gate, visitors move from God to the Godless, in the Ripon Prison and Police Museum. Housed in the cell block of what was first the Ripon Liberty Prison and later its Police Station, the museum tells the vivid story of Yorkshire law and disorder through the ages. It has some chilling but never gruesome displays. It's one of a series of sites making up the Yorkshire Law and Order Museums. The city's Law and Order Trail will also take you to the Old Workhouse Museum and the Courthouse Museum.

All around Ripon attractions vie for attention. The Lightwater Valley Theme Park, with its enormous roller-coasters and other rides, is high on the list for families. There are, naturally, lots of eating places and gift shops, and the Lightwater Village, a shopping centre with factory, fashion and food shops.

■ Activity

VIA FERRATA

One of only two dedicated Via Ferrata in England (the phrase is Italian for 'Iron Way'), the How Stean Gorge Experience connects a series of rope ladders, bridges and abseils along this dramatic gorge. It's part gorge walk, part rock scramble. Accompanied by expert guides, it's wet, exhilarating and enormous fun. Booking is essential. Contact How Stean Gorge Outdoor Centre (www.howstean.co.uk).

■ Insight

SOUND TRADITIONS

Every night at 9pm the Ripon Hornblower blows his horn in the market place and then once more outside the home of the mayor. The ceremony marks the setting of the watch, informing the citizens that their safekeeping overnight was the charge of the wakeman. The office of wakeman disappeared in 1604, but the tradition lives on. Also at 9pm, the curfew bell at Ripon Cathedral is sounded (unless a concert is taking place). This custom comes from the Normans, when it was an instruction that all fires should be covered for the night – a safety precaution in the days of timber houses. The word curfew comes from the French, *couvre-feu* – 'cover the fire'.

Just 2 miles (3.2km) east of Lightwater Valley is Norton Conyers, a lovely country house which dates back to the mid-14th century. Visitors will hear the legend of the Mad Woman, a story also heard by Charlotte Brontë when she visited the house in 1839. The character in the novel possibly inspired the mad Mrs Rochester in *Jane Eyre*, written eight years later, but there are other claimants to this honour.

To Small Towns and Large Villages

Middleham, with its market, splendid Norman castle and horse-racing stables, is the smallest town in the Yorkshire Dales – much smaller than many villages. This drive takes in some of the attractive places that hover between town and village, such as Kettlewell, Grassington, Leyburn and Pateley Bridge, where the tour starts, and some of the finest scenery the Dales have to offer.

Route Directions

The drive starts in Pateley Bridge, a lively market town in the heart of Nidderdale with its own fascinating local museum, shopping and Tourist Information Centre.

1 From the centre of Pateley Bridge take the minor road that leads north from near the bridge itself, towards Ramsgill and Lofthouse. Pass Gouthwaite Reservoir on your right. In Lofthouse turn right and take the steep road out of the village, over the moors towards Masham. Continue for about 6 miles (9.7km), passing two more reservoirs on the right. Take the third left turning, as you approach Healey, towards Ellingstring. Turn left at the crossroads, continue to the junction with the A6108 and turn left to Leyburn passing the remains of Jervaulx Abbey, right. Founded in 1156, the abbey is in complete contrast to grand and busy Fountains Abbey, yet in its day Jervaulx was one of the most important Cistercian abbeys in Yorkshire.

2 Continue on the A6108 and pass through Middleham. Middleham is considered to be 'the Newmarket of the north', with its 16 or so racing stables. The impressive castle ruins was the much-favoured home of King Richard III, whose son Edward was born here in 1473.

3 Continue to Leyburn, a busy Wensleydale town with many tea shops for visitors as well as a wealth of everyday shops. In Leyburn turn left then right following signs 'A6108 Richmond'. Through Bellerby, turn right then left, still with the A6108. The road first takes you over upland pasture then along the wooded Alpine-like slopes of Swaledale towards Richmond. At this point you can choose to take a detour and continue into Richmond, which stands at the foot of Swaledale.
Richmond's castle commands an impressive position above the river. The town has a large cobbled square, a

church with shops in its side, riverside walks and three good museums.

4 If you are not taking the detour, continue as before and as you reach Richmond pass a right turn to Catterick, turn immediately left up Hurgill Road, past a car park on the left. This road takes you back along the Swale but climbs high above the river, before dropping steeply down to Marske. Cross the bridge and turn right towards Reeth, then turn left on to the B6270 to Grinton. In Grinton turn right on to a minor road and take the right fork following the signs for Redmire. You are now on an impressive high moorland road passing disused lead mines. When the road finally descends, take the first turning on the right for the village of Castle Bolton then turn right for Carperby. Take a left turn to visit Aysgarth Falls – a very popular beauty spot.
Although they consist of three different sections, only the

Upper Falls are visible from the road. Near by are a mill, a carriage museum and tea rooms, while Aysgarth village itself is another half-mile (800m) away, on the main Wensleydale road.

5 Beyond Aysgarth Falls turn left on to the A684 signposted Leyburn and then take the second turning on the right on to the B6160 following the signs into West Burton. This has been described as the prettiest village in the Dales. It has a large village green, on which horses graze and children play. There is a pub and a pottery, but no church or market. Burton Force waterfall is a short stroll away.

6 Rejoin the B6160 to drive along the lovely Bishopdale, and over Kidstones Pass to Buckden in Wharfedale. Pass Kettlewell on the left. Kettlewell is small town and a centre for walkers tackling nearby Great Whernside. It is also on the Dales Way long-distance footpath, and was once a centre of the lead-mining industry.

7 Continue ahead and look out for Kilnsey Crag on your right, easily identified as it juts out dramatically towards the main road.

Kilnsey Crag is popular with climbers, film-makers and peregrine falcons.

8 Continue on the B6160 then turn left to reach the centre of Grassington. This is an attractive, large village with cobbled streets,

17th- and 18th-century houses, pubs and a museum of Upper Wharfedale life.

9 Drive around the centre of Grassington, and leave on the B6265 and then make the return journey to Nidderdale and Pateley Bridge.

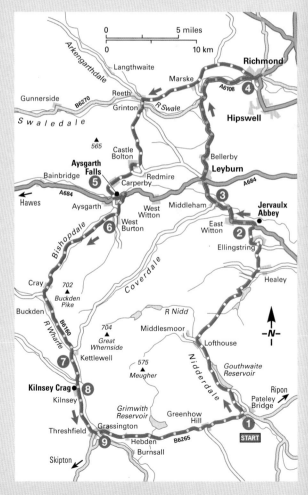

A Circuit from Lofthouse

A walk from Lofthouse to Ramsgill and Middlesmoor in the valley of the River Nidd, enjoying the rich farmland and moorland landscape. Nidderdale is a designated Area of Outstanding Natural Beauty. In the 19th and 20th centuries parts of the dale were dammed as a chain of reservoirs was constructed to supply water to Bradford.

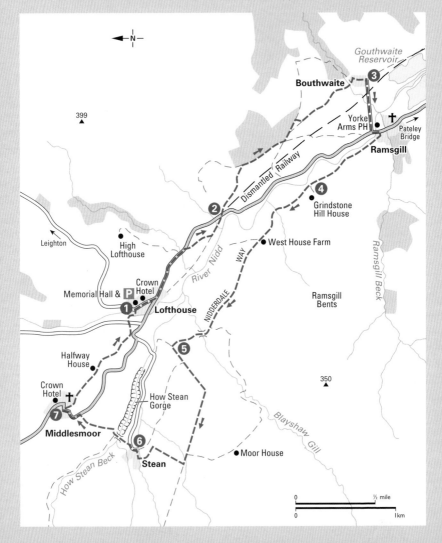

Route Directions

1 Walk downhill past the Crown Hotel. At the main road turn left. Just beyond the track to High Lofthouse farm go right, through a stile. Follow a clear track bending left to a waymarked stile, then bear left to another stile. Continue down to a slightly raised track (the old railway) and bear left to rejoin the road.

2 Cross the road and go through a gate, signed Bouthwaite. Bear left off the farm track to a stile and ascend a grassy ramp. Bear left to climb more steeply, then right towards a plantation. Follow a clear path just below the plantation. Pass a house then join a track and follow it past a gate and Nidderdale Way sign to a fork. Bear left, still parallel to the plantation, then turn right over a stile. Descend left of a farmhouse, then bear left to a tall ladder stile. Walk straight ahead, keep a wall to your right and descend into a wooded valley. Ignore a stile on the right and go through a waymarked gate, over a wooden bridge, through a metal gate and ahead. Bear right past a house down a gravelled track to a lane.

3 Turn right down the lane to a T-junction. Turn left, over the bridge. Turn right by the triangular green, then right again, signed 'Stean'. Follow the track until it bends left up to Grindstone Hill House.

4 Go straight on, over four stiles. At West House Farm go over a stile between the farm and a bungalow, cross the farm road, follow waymarked posts (Nidderdale Way) and continue along a track, eventually descending to a signpost near a barn. Follow the obvious track into a valley and over a bridge.

5 At a T-junction of tracks, turn left. Follow the walled track uphill, bending right. As the main track bends left to Moor House, keep straight on along a grassy track. Another track joins from the left. Just beyond this, after crossing a stream, turn right. Bend left by a farm and follow the track over a ford into Stean.

6 Follow the lane right, then take a stile on the left signed 'Middlesmoor'. Descend into How Stean Gorge, down steps, over a bridge and up steps, then follow signs to the road. Turn left into Middlesmoor. Turn right beside the Wesleyan chapel to the gateway of the parish church.

7 Turn right before the gate, through a stile signed 'Lofthouse'. Follow the path to Halfway House farm. Go through the farmyard to a gate and follow the right side of two fields then bear left across the third to a gate in the corner. In the lay-by go left through a gate, then along the path beside the cricket ground. Cross the lane and go over a bridge, then bear right to emerge near the Market Cross in Lofthouse. Turn left to the car park.

Route facts

DISTANCE/TIME 7 miles (11.3km) 3h

MAP OS Explorer OL30 Yorkshire Dales – Northern & Central

START Car park by Memorial Hall in Lofthouse, grid ref: SE 101734

TRACKS Mostly field paths and tracks, may be muddy, 18 stiles

GETTING TO THE START Lofthouse lies near the end of the Nidderdale road, 6 miles (9.7km) northwest of Pateley Bridge.

THE PUB Crown Hotel, Middlesmoor. Tel: 01423 755204

❶ A long walk for young children

■ TOURIST INFORMATION CENTRES

Harrogate
Royal Baths, Crescent Road.
Tel: 0845 389 3223
Knaresborough
9 Castle Courtyard.
Tel: 0845 389 0177
Pateley Bridge
18 High Street.
Tel: 0845 389 0179
Ripon
Minster Road.
Tel: 0845 389 0178

■ PARKING

Limited free disc parking is
available in Harrogate, Ripon
and Knaresborough, usually
up to two hours. Discs can be
obtained from TICs, shops,
banks, etc. Car parking is
difficult in Knaresborough,
and you are advised to use
pay-and-display car parks.

■ PLACES OF INTEREST

Brimham Rocks
Southwest of Brimham off
the B6265.
Tel: 01423 780688
**Fountains Abbey and Studley
Royal Water Garden**
Ripon. Tel: 01765 608888
World Heritage Site managed
by the National Trust.
**Harrogate Turkish Baths
and Health Spa**
Parliament Street,
Harrogate.
Tel: 01423 556746

How Stean Gorge
near Lofthouse, Pateley
Bridge. Tel: 01423 755666
Knaresborough Castle
Tel: 01423 556188
Marmion Tower
West Tanfield, Ripon. Free.
Mercer Art Gallery
Swan Road, Harrogate.
Tel: 01423 556188
Mother Shipton's Cave
Knaresborough.
Tel: 01423 864600
Newby Hall and Gardens
Ripon. Tel: 0845 450 4068;
www.newbyhall.com
Nidderdale Museum
Millfield Street, Pateley
Bridge. Tel: 01423 711225
Norton Conyers
Ripon. Tel: 01765 640333
Old Courthouse Museum
Castle Yard, Knaresborough.
Tel: 01423 556188
RHS Garden Harlow Carr
Crag Lane, Otley Road,
Harrogate.
Tel: 01423 565418;
www.rhs.org.uk
Ripley Castle
Ripley.
Tel: 01423 770152
Ripon Law & Order Museums
Ripon Museum Trust,
The Workhouse Museum,
Allhallowgate.
Tel: 01765 690799;
www.riponmuseums.co.uk
Royal Pump Room Museum
Royal Parade, Harrogate.
Tel: 01423 556188

Stump Cross Caverns
Between Pateley Bridge and
Grassington. On B6265 west
of Pateley Bridge.
Tel: 01756 752780

■ FOR CHILDREN

**Lightwater Valley Theme
Park and Village**
North Stainley, Ripon.
Tel: 0871 720 0011

■ SHOPPING

Harrogate
Large shopping centre and
mall, including the Victoria
Shopping Centre. Harrogate
is good for antiques,
second-hand books and
clothes.
Knaresborough
Open-air market, Wed.
The Lightwater Village
Next to Lightwater Valley
Theme Park, is a shopping
centre with factory outlets.
Ripon
Open-air market, Thu.

■ LOCAL SPECIALITIES

Clocks
Philip Oliver, Finkle Street,
Knaresborough.
Tel: 01423 868438
Craft Workshops
King Street Workshops, King
Street, Pateley Bridge; www.
kingstreetworkshops.co.uk.
Several craft workshops,
including pottery, jewellery
and glassblowing.

Pottery

Littlethorpe Potteries,
Littlethorpe, Ripon.
Tel: 01765 603786
Country pottery using local
clay, with pot-throwing
demonstrations.

Yorkshire Country Wines

Riverside Cellars, The Mill,
Glasshouses, Harrogate.
Tel: 01423 711947/711223

■ PERFORMING ARTS

Harrogate Theatre

Oxford Street, Harrogate.
Tel: 01423 502116;
www.harrogatetheatre.co.uk

■ OUTDOOR ACTIVITIES & SPORTS

ANGLING

Fly

Pateley Bridge Scar House
Dam. Day tickets from
Lofthouse Post Office.
Tel: 01423 755203
Also check 'Where to fish' on
www.harrogate.gov.uk

BOAT HIRE

Knaresborough

Blenkhorns Boat Hire,
2 Waterside, High Bridge.
Tel: 01423 862105
Rowing boats, punts and
canoes for hire.

HORSE-RACING

Ripon

2 miles (3.2km) southeast of
Ripon on B6265.
Tel: 01765 530530;
www.ripon-races.co.uk

HORSE-RIDING

Pateley Bridge

Bewerley School of
Horsemanship, Bewerley Old
Hall. Tel: 01423 712249

Markington

Yorkshire Riding Centre.
Tel: 01765 677207;
www.yrc.co.uk

LONG-DISTANCE FOOTPATHS & TRAILS

Nidderdale Way

This 53-mile (85km) walk
tours the moors and gritstone
outcrops of the lovely valley
of Nidderdale, starting and
finishing in Pateley Bridge.

The Yorkshire Water Way

The first 41-mile (66km)
section of this reservoir-
themed walk enters Upper
Nidderdale from Kettlewell,
before crossing over to the
Washburn Valley on its way
to Ilkley.

■ EVENTS & CUSTOMS

Fountains Abbey

Egg-rolling, Easter Mon.

Harrogate

Harrogate International
Youth Music Festival, held
every Easter, with
performances throughout
the region including Ripon
Cathedral.
Spring Flower Show, late Apr.
Northern Antiques Show,
early May.
The Great Yorkshire Show,
mid-Jul.

Harrogate International
Festival, late Jul to early Aug.
Trans-Pennine Run for
vintage vehicles from
Manchester to Harrogate,
early Aug.
Autumn Flower Show,
mid-Sep.

Knaresborough

Knaresborough Bed Race,
early Jun.
Knaresborough Festival of
Entertainment and Visual Art
(FEVA), mid-Aug.

Middlesmoor

Bell Festival, Jun.

Pateley Bridge

Nidderdale Show, late Sep,
held in Bewerley Park.

Ripley

Ripley Show, mid-Aug.

Ripon

Setting the Watch by the
Ripon Hornblower every
evening in the market place
by the Obelisk at 9pm.
Every Thu at 11am the Ripon
Bellringer declares the
market open.
International Festival,
mid-Sep.
Ripon Spring Festival, late
May to early Jun.
St Wilfrid's Feast Procession,
Sat before the first Mon, Aug.

Tea Rooms

Bettys
1 Parliament Street,
Harrogate HG1 2QU
Tel: 01423 814070;
www.bettys.co.uk
The story of this noble
Yorkshire institution began
here in 1919, and you can still
enjoy more than 50 teas and
coffees and over 300 breads,
cakes and chocolates. The
glorious art nouveau interior
was designed by Charles
Spindler's studio in Alsace
in the 1930s.

The Old Granary
Tea Shop
17 High Street, Pateley
Bridge, Harrogate HG3 5AP
Tel: 01423 711852
In the centre of this delightful
village, you'll find that the
Granary is perfect for a quick
bite or a light lunch. As well
as various teas and coffees,
the tasty home-made apple
crumble is popular. There are
a few restaurant evenings.

How Stean Gorge Café
Lofthouse, Pateley Bridge
HG3 5SF. Tel: 01423 755666;
www.howstean.co.uk
The tea room serves up
'traditional Yorkshire grub' –
roast beef and Yorkshire
pudding is a speciality, but
the raspberry pavlovas have
also acquired a following.

Delicious cakes and aromatic
freshly ground coffee may
also tempt you to linger here.

Miller's Cottage
Darley Mill, Darley,
Harrogate HG3 2QQ
Tel: 01423 780857
After a gruelling session of
bargain hunting at this mill
shop, the Miller's Cottage is
perfect for winding down and
discussing your purchases.
Delicious home-made cakes,
biscuits and light snacks, or
even a spot of lunch can be
enjoyed in this delightful old
cottage in Harrogate.

Pubs

Bridge Inn
Low Wath Road, Pateley
Bridge, Harrogate HG3 5HL
Tel: 01423 711484
The Bridge may look like a
traditional Dales pub, but it
has only been in open since
2003. In that short time it has
established a good reputation
for excellent, locally sourced
food and reliable beers.

Sportsman's Arms
Wath-in-Nidderdale, Pateley
Bridge, Harrogate HG3 5PP
Tel: 01423 711306
A custom-built kitchen lies at
the heart of this up-market
watering hole, where local
fish and game vie with fresh
deliveries from Whitby and

locally sourced beef, lamb
and pork in the softly lit,
wicker-backed chaired dining
room. The 140-bin wine list
skilfully complements the
menu, while the bar area
retains the ambience of an
important and busy hub of
the rural community.

Crown Hotel
Middlesmoor, Pateley Bridge
HG3 5ST. Tel: 01423 755204
Nearly 1,000 foot (305m)
up, towards the head of
Nidderdale, Middlesmoor,
with the Crown Hotel at its
core, commands a fine view
down the valley and over
Gouthwaite Reservoir. The
pub is homely, family-run and
serves up a range of reliable
food and good Black Sheep
beer – traditional Sunday
lunches are very popular. In
sunny weather, you can eat
outside in the garden.

Royal Oak
36 Kirkgate, Ripon HG4 1PB
Tel: 01765 602284
The Royal Oak is just a few
steps away from Ripon's
Market Square, and just
around the corner from the
cathedral. Expect tasty,
freshly cooked food to be
served every lunchtime, from
a 'salad or chips' style menu,
and the beer is from Timothy
Taylor's of Keighley.

Central Dales

This is the real heart of the Dales. It has the highest peaks – Ingleborough, Whernside, Pen-y-ghent and Buckden Pike – the biggest caverns, including the exciting White Scar Caves, potholes galore and attractive villages and towns, little-touched, it seems, by the worst aspects of modern times. It is a landscape both rolling and rugged, a landscape, that is truly perfect for walkers, for climbers, for cavers and for fell runners – those who like their scenery to have a challenge about it. But it also has plenty to offer visitors, who are content to marvel at the grandeur of it all from lesser altitudes.

CUMBRIA

Kendal

Sedbergh

Swaledale

713 Great Shunner Fell

Leyburn

Wensleydale

Hawes

Aysgarth

Barbon

686 Craghill 736

Whernside

667 Dodd Fell

YORKSHIRE

Kearstwick

Kirkby Lonsdale

Whittington

Chapel le Dale

Langstrothdale Chase

6 Cray 702 Buckden Pike

DALES

Hubberholme

605 Little Whernside

Thornton in Lonsdale

Tunstall

723

Ingleton

Selside

Halton Gill

693 Pen-y-Ghent

NATIONAL

Litton

704 Great Whernside

Ingleborough

Horton in Ribblesdale

PARK

Arncliffe

5 Kettlewell

575 Meugher

Burton in Lonsdale

Austwick Studfold

Hawkswick

High Bentham Clapham

Kilnsey Conistone

Grimwith Reservoir

Settle

Threshfield Grassington

Hebden

Forest of Bowland

Skipton

Ilkley

LANCASHIRE

Clitheroe

Colne

Keighley

5 Walk start point

GRASSINGTON

Unmissable attractions

If you're feeling reasonably fit, climb to the summit of Pen-y-ghent for views across to the other peaks...or Whernside, the highest point in the Dales...explore Clapham, one of the prettiest villages with Clapham Beck running through its centre...discover Barden Tower, southeast of Grassington, a medieval hunting lodge that was renovated by Lady Anne Clifford, a name you will encounter throughout the Dales... wander around Kirkby Lonsdale, just over the border in Cumbria, an unspoiled place whose charms have been recognised over the years by artists and authors.

1 Kettlewell
The charming village of Kettlewell is surrounded by rich valley pastures divided by drystone walls. In the distance are the slopes of Great Whernside.

2 Ruskin's View
A lovely sweeping view of the Lune Valley, just beyond St Mary's churchyard in Kirkby Lonsdale, as painted by J M W Turner in 1818.

3 Pen-y-ghent
A path of wooden boards, keeping walkers above the boggy fells, leads towards distinctive Pen-y-ghent, the third highest of Yorkshire's Three Peaks.

4 Grassington
A terrace of typical stone cottages, fronted by troughs of pretty flowers, line a cobbled street in Grassington.

5 Ribblesdale
Traditional stone walls in the foreground of a misty Ribblesdale landscape – one of the quieter areas in the National Park.

CLAPHAM MAP REF SD7469

Clapham is one of the prettiest little villages that anyone could wish to find; it is almost as if it was planned with the picture postcard in mind. A stream, Clapham Beck, runs through its centre, crossed by old stone bridges, and matching old stone cottages line its narrow lanes. It is much more wooded than most villages in the Dales, which adds to its appeal, and with several guest houses and cafés, a pub, a nature trail and a couple of shops for essential supplies, it makes an excellent base for exploring the southern part of this area.

The Ingleborough Estate Nature Trail celebrates one of Clapham's well-known sons, Reginald Farrer, who spent his time collecting plant species from all around the world and cultivating them here, on the family estate. He died in 1920, before he was 40, but by that time he had become one of Britain's leading botanical experts and earned himself the name of 'the father of English rock gardening'. The trail, which goes past an ornamental lake and then through a wooded valley, leads to Ingleborough Cave, where guided tours of almost an hour take visitors into the network of caves below Ingleborough, which include what is said to be the longest stalactite in the country, at 16 feet 5 inches (5m).

For such a small place, Clapham has several claims to fame. The limestone caves have been open to visitors since 1838, when a stalagmite barrier 70 feet (21m) into the cave was breached giving access to the labyrinth beyond. Since then, modern cave-diving techniques have allowed links to be made as far as Gaping Gill. Another local man was James Faraday, the village blacksmith and father of Michael Faraday, the great physicist and chemist who formulated Faraday's Law on electrolysis and whose discoveries led to the invention of the dynamo, the motor and refrigeration.

■ Visit

THE NORBER BOULDERS

Follow the bridleway between Clapham and Austwick and you will see a signpost to the Norber Boulders. This scattering of boulders, each on its own little pedestal of rock, at first glance looks as if it ought to be of some human significance, but in fact it is a natural occurrence. The boulders, also called the Norber Erratics, are several hundred million years old and were deposited in their present location by the actions of a glacier about 25,000 years ago. They are made of Silurian gritstone, the type of rock found in Crummack Dale about half a mile (800m) to the north.

■ Insight

THE WITCH OF CLAPHAM

Dame Alice Ketyll, a Clapham inhabitant in the mid-15th century, was an unusual witch in that she was popular with the villagers, using her strange powers for their benefit wherever possible. Inevitably, she was less popular with the Church – an ecclesiastical court tried her for witchcraft and punished her by demanding that she line the roof of the village church with lead. Dame Alice could not afford to buy the lead, so she took a party of clerics and workmen to Ingleborough where they found both lead and silver. The silver paid for the men to take the lead and line the church roof, and Dame Alice's reward for this ingenuity was that she could be buried in the churchyard.

GRASSINGTON   MAP REF SE0063

Grassington may look as if it has always been a small and sleepy Dales town, but this is not the case. With the discovery of large and valuable lead deposits on the surrounding moors, it became a thriving industrial town from the 17th to the 19th centuries, so much so that by the early 1800s it was noted for its drunken and violent nature. The arrival of Methodism did much to improve matters, and two large Georgian-style chapels still survive in the village, although one is now a Congregational church.

Modern Grassington is the major tourist centre in Upper Wharfedale, with a large number of guest houses, shops and eating places radiating out from its cobbled market square. It also has a National Park Centre, near the village centre, and the Upper Wharfedale Folk Museum, a tiny but enjoyable collection housed in two 18th-century former lead-miners' cottages, which explores the history of mining in the area.

Five miles (8km) southeast, off the B6160 road, is Appletreewick village, a pretty place where the hillside Parcevall Hall Gardens, which were laid out from 1927, are planted with specimen trees and shrubs from western China and the Himalayas. The gardens have fine formal terraces, a glorious rose garden, rock garden, woodland walks, orchards, a 15th-century farmhouse and wonderful views of Wharfedale.

Six miles (9.7km) to the southeast of Grassington on the B6160, is Barden Tower, a medieval hunting lodge that was renovated and used by Lady Anne Clifford in the mid-17th century. Lady

■ Visit

BRITAIN'S WILD WEST

Situated close to the Ribblehead Viaduct are just a few trenches, which are all that remain of Batty Green. This was the name that was given to the village of wooden huts that housed up to 2,000 workmen in the 1870s, when they were working on the Settle–Carlisle Railway line. There are interpretative panels by the site and a further display in the station. Batty Green and other shanty-towns were Britain's own Wild West in Victorian times, with saloons, religious missions, good-time girls and fearsome reputations.

Anne was an admirable woman whose name you will encounter throughout the Yorkshire Dales. Her father was the Earl of Cumberland, who died when Anne was 15 years old, but instead of inheriting his estate as the Earl's only child, he bequeathed it all, including his vast lands in Cumberland, Westmorland and Yorkshire, to his brother and then to his brother's son. Lady Anne fought all her life to regain her inheritance, which she eventually did when her cousin died without heirs. She put her wealth to good use, building charitable institutions and renovating buildings, including Barden Tower. She also restored Brougham Castle at Penrith in Cumbria, where she died in 1676 at the age of 86. The Lady Anne Clifford Trail, established in 1990, commemorates the 400th anniversary of her birth in Skipton Castle, where the trail begins. This 100-mile (161km) long-distance path leads all the way through the Yorkshire Dales and the Upper Eden Valley to Brougham Castle.

HORTON IN RIBBLESDALE

MAP REF SD8071

The kind of village that straggles along a main road, Horton in Ribblesdale is easily missed but it is an important place for many visitors to the area. It sits surrounded by the Dales Three Peaks – Pen-y-ghent, Whernside and Ingleborough, and the Three Peaks Challenge Race starts and ends here every year. The Pen-y-ghent Café has become an important centre for walkers, particularly for the very efficient safety system it operates, allowing walkers to clock out and clock back in again at the end of the day.

The Pennine Way weaves its way through Horton in Ribblesdale, which also has a station on the Settle–Carlisle line. One of the big attractions nearby is the Ribblehead Viaduct, a major triumph of engineering, with 24 arches rising to 165 feet (50m) above the valley floor.

HUBBERHOLME   MAP REF SD9278

With its riverside setting, surrounded by trees in the valley floor, there are fewer more picturesque villages to be found than Hubberholme. It is not surprising, then, to discover that it was the favourite place of J B Priestley. This Bradford author, who wrote *The Good Companions* and many other books and stage plays, loved Hubberholme and visited it often. He drank in the village pub, and a plaque in the local church commemorates his great affection for the tiny village where he chose his ashes to be scattered.

The Church of St Michael and All Angels, one of the delights of the Dales, was originally a chapel in the Norman hunting forest of Langstrothdale Chase. A major attraction is its rood loft from 1558, which only survives thanks to Hubberholme's isolation. In 1571 an edict was issued in the York Diocese to destroy all rood lofts in the region, but Hubberholme's was one of only two in Yorkshire to escape destruction. Look also for the mouse symbol of Robert Thompson, the 'Mouseman', who made much of the church's more recent woodwork. The work of this furniture maker, from Kilburn in Yorkshire, is distinguished by a tiny mouse carved somewhere on the piece.

INGLEBOROUGH   MAP REF SD7494

There are several ways of approaching Ingleborough on foot, from Clapham, Ingleton, Horton in Ribblesdale and Chapel-le-Dale, and each is an energetic but rewarding climb to the top of the peak's 2,372 feet (723m). Until accurate measurement of hills became possible, Ingleborough was long believed to be the highest point in Yorkshire. We now know that it is surpassed by both Whernside and Mickle Fell (now in County Durham). At its top is a wide plateau, with a triangulation point and a stone windbreak, and of course grand views all around. An Iron Age fort once stood here, and horse races have been run in more recent memory, with bonfires still lit occasionally for special celebrations.

The path from Chapel-le-Dale is the shortest and steepest approach, giving a daunting impression of the challenge to come as you look up at Ingleborough's imposing heights. From Clapham the walk is about 4 miles (6.4km) one-way, passing Ingleborough Cave on the way. Ingleborough's slopes have a great number of potholes, so you need to take care if you stray from the path. Anywhere that is fenced off will be like that for a purpose, so don't let curiosity get the better of you.

South of the summit of Ingleborough you'll see the Gaping Gill pothole, though to describe it as a pothole is like calling Westminster Abbey a parish church. In fact you could probably fit the abbey inside Gaping Gill: some mathematician has certainly worked out that you can fit York Minster Cathedral inside the main cavern. This is about 120 feet (37m) high and 500 feet (152m) long, and down into it from the surface the stream of Fell Beck plunges, making it one of the highest waterfalls in Britain at 364 feet (111m). The breathtaking sight of the interior of Gaping Gill is normally reserved for experienced potholers, but twice a year, on Spring and Summer Bank Holidays, local caving clubs set up a winch and bosun's chair and allow members of the public to share the event.

INGLETON MAP REF SD6973

Ingleton has too much modern sprawl to be called a pretty village, but it has an attractive centre with steep winding streets going down to the gorge where its celebrated Waterfalls Walk starts. Before the arrival of the railway in the late 19th century, bringing the visitors and walkers who heralded much of the new development, Ingleton relied on its woollen and cotton spinning industries, and before that coal mining and stone

quarrying. Now instead of mill-workers' cottages there are guest houses, shops and several pubs, though the rock quarry is still one of the largest in the Dales.

The Church of St Mary the Virgin is in a dominating position in the village, and has been rebuilt several times over the centuries, though the 15th-century tower remains. Its oldest feature is a Norman font, carved with figures from the life of Christ, which was rediscovered in 1830, having been hidden in the river below for safe-keeping during times of religious persecution. The church also boasts what is known as the 'Vinegar Bible', so-called because of a misprint in 1717 in what should have been the Parable of the Vineyards.

On the B6255 to the northeast of Ingleton is the White Scar Cave, the best show cave in the Dales. With rivers and waterfalls, these make for exhilarating subterranean guided tours.

■ Activity

THE THREE PEAKS CHALLENGE

First completed in 1887, this walk traditionally starts at the Pen-y-ghent Café in Horton in Ribblesdale, where a safety system of checking everyone in and out operates. The route takes walkers to the top of Ingleborough, Whernside and Pen-y-ghent. That first walk took 10 hours, although anyone who finishes the 25-mile (40.2km) route in under 12 hours is then eligible to membership in the Three Peaks of Yorkshire Club. If an average speed of only 2mph (3.2kph) doesn't seem very fast, remember that the total height of the Three Peaks, each of which must be ascended on the walk, is over 7,000 feet (2,150m), and so it is not a challenge to be undertaken lightly.

From Arncliffe to Kettlewell

A walk through rocky hillside, moorland and meadows from Arncliffe to Kettlewell, returning alongside the River Skirfare. Arncliffe sits spectacularly on a great spit of gravel above the floodplain of the river. Before the building of the bridge, a ford allowed travellers an easy crossing for the many ancient tracks that converge here.

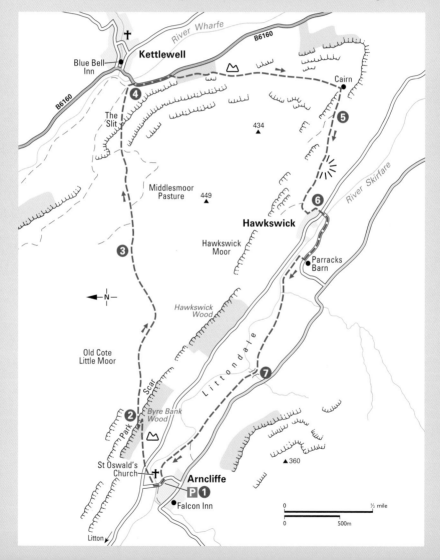

Route Directions

1 From the car park, cross the bridge and turn immediately right, over a gated stile. Walk parallel with the river, cross the road via two stiles, then bear right and follow the footpath uphill over a stile and through a gate. Continue up in the same direction through the woods of Park Scar, with one short zig-zag near the top, to a stile.

2 Bear right and follow the footpath to another stile. Keep on the same heading to pass a signpost, a tumbled wall and then another signpost. The path bears left, crosses a line of shakeholes and continues via a stile to another stile on the ridge.

3 Descend on the same heading. The path passes more shakeholes and descends beside a wall to a ladder stile. Follow the path down, descending steeply to a signpost. Cross a track and reach another signpost above a limestone scar overlooking Kettlewell. Descend a narrow cleft (The Slit), then descend to a track. Turn right and walk to the road.

4 Turn right for 300yds (274m), then go right through a gate by a fingerpost, bearing right again at another sign.

Climb through woodland, go through a gate, then bear right and up to a small ruin. Continue along the edge of trees and round to a gateway beside a stile. Bear left to another stile then ascend the grassy path, keeping right where it forks, along a broad shelf. Eventually reach another stile and begin to descend, bending right by a cairn.

5 At a track junction continue ahead, with a wall on your left. The track leads down into Hawkswick village. On the outskirts go left, curve right between buildings and descend to the lane.

6 Cross the bridge and follow the lane round right. Just before farm buildings on the left, turn right towards a footbridge; turn left before it at the 'Arncliffe' sign. Follow the river to a footbridge over a side-stream and continue to a double gate. The path bears slightly away from the river to a gate. Cross the field beyond, skirting a steep bank above the river, to reach another footbridge.

7 Walk past a barn and through a gate, then bear left to a squeeze stile and cross a track. From the next stile

Route facts

DISTANCE/TIME 6.5 miles (10.4km) 3h30

MAP OS Explorer OL30 Yorkshire Dales – Northern & Central

START Arncliffe, near church, grid ref: SD 932719.

TRACKS Mostly clear, some rocky sections, may be muddy, 16 stiles

GETTING TO THE START Turn north from the A59 near Skipton along the B6160 Grassington road. Turn left just beyond Kilnsey for Arncliffe. Limited parking near church and around village green.

THE PUB Blue Bell Inn, Kettlewell. Tel: 01756 760230; www.bluebellkettlewell. co.uk

❶ Steep, slippery limestone section above Arncliffe. Navigation in hill fog could be difficult – save for settled weather. A very short steep descent (Point 3)

bear slightly right to rejoin the river. Follow the path, with plentiful waymarks and signs, to emerge by the churchyard and return to the start point.

Along Langstrothdale from Hubberholme

A route from author J B Priestley's favourite Dales village, along Langstrothdale Chase, a Norman hunting ground that had its own forest laws and punishments. You then walk along a typical limestone terrace to reach Cray and follow the Cray Gill downstream past a series of small cascades. (For a more spectacular waterfall, head up the road a little distance to Cray High Bridge.) Literary pilgrims visit the village of Hubberholme to see The George Inn, where Priestley could often be found enjoying the local ale, and the churchyard the last resting place for his ashes. He chose an idyllic spot, Hubberholme is a cluster of old farmhouses and cottages surrounding the Church of St Michael and All Angels.

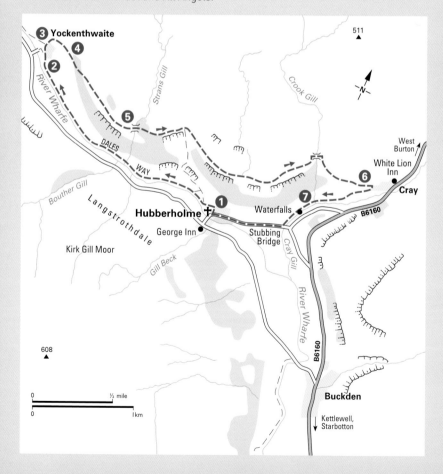

Route Directions

1 Enter the farmyard beside the church and turn left immediately through a Dales Way signed gate. Take the lower path, signed 'Yockenthwaite', alongside the churchyard. Walk beside the river for 1.25 miles (2km); the clear Dales Way path is never far from the river. Approaching Yockenthwaite, go up steps to a little gate and left to a gate and signpost.

2 Follow the track towards a bridge but, before reaching it, go sharp right up a farm track, which swings back left to a sign to Cray and Hubberholme.

3 Go up to another signpost, then follow the obvious track slanting right and up. Part-way up the hill, go right at a footpath sign through a gate.

4 Follow the near-level path to a signpost, then bear left and up a rough section to another signpost. Turn right and follow the obvious path, descending along a beautiful natural terrace until the path goes left and up to enter a wood by a footbridge over a miniature gorge.

5 Walk through the wood then continue, level again, to reach a small side valley above a house. A signpost above the house points towards Cray. Go up slightly, over rocks, then along another green terrace path for about a mile (1.6km) to a footbridge. Cross this, then ascend slightly to a barn; bear right to a gate then follow a marked path across meadow land. Go past a house to a junction of tracks on the edge of Cray.

6 Go sharp right, down to a footpath sign to Stubbing Bridge. Descend between stone walls and through a gate and on to the grassy hillside. Pass another footpath sign and continue downhill to meet the stream.

7 Follow the streamside path past waterfalls and pools, crossing a stone bridge over a side-stream. Cross a stile and continue past a barn to reach the road. Turn right back to the parking place in Hubberholme.

Extending the walk

You can see more of the beautiful Upper Wharfedale scenery by extending the walk from Cray to the peaceful village of Buckden. From Point 6 on the main walk, follow a metalled road to the White Lion Inn, then cross the valley and climb to Buckden Rake. Descend this to Buckden before returning to the car parking place at Hubberholme via the Dales Way.

Route facts

DISTANCE/TIME 5.25 miles (8.4km) 2h

MAP OS Explorer OL30 Yorkshire Dales – Northern & Central

START Beside river in Hubberholme, opposite church (not church parking), grid ref: SD 927782.

TRACKS Field paths and tracks, steep after Yockenthwaite, 11 stiles

GETTING TO THE START The tiny little village of Hubberholme is situated in Upper Wharfedale 18 miles (29km) north of Skipton. From the A59 Skipton bypass, follow the B6160 north. In Buckden turn left along a narrow country lane for Hubberholme. Cross the bridge by The George Inn, where there is roadside parking by the river.

THE PUB The George Inn, Hubberholme. Tel: 01756 760223; www.thegeorge-inn.co.uk

KETTLEWELL MAP REF SD9772

The main Wharfedale road scarcely touches the village, so much of Kettlewell remains a tranquil retreat of charming 17th- and 18th-century houses. It was once a more important place than it is today; it received its market charter back in the 13th century, and Fountains and Coverham abbeys and Bolton Priory all owned tracts of land near by. Later there were flourishing lead-mining and local textile industries too, which helped create those charming houses.

Kettlewell's past is full of interesting stories. In 1218 its parson was cruelly murdered, the deed believed to have been done by a man who had taken the parson's mistress and stolen her away to Skipton. A later parson turned part of his house into an inn, to supplement his meagre stipend.

When abbeys such as Fountains and Jervaulx were at their prime, they owned vast amounts of land in the Yorkshire Dales. They built granges in some of the further places, as bases, and these were connected to the abbey by the equivalent of a drovers' road, allowing large flocks of sheep to be moved aound the estates. Many of these roads are still in use as paths and bridleways, an example being Mastiles Lane, which starts in Malham, and goes all the way across Mastiles and Kilnsey Moor, to emerge at the Wharfe near Kilnsey. Kilnsey Old Hall, once a grange for Fountains Abbey, is today used as holiday accommodation.

Kilnsey Crag, a bulbous limestone bulge that looms ominously towards the main road, attracts both climbers and film-makers. It stands 170 feet (52m)

high, with a 40-foot (12m) overhang. Near by you'll find Kilnsey Park, with trout-fishing ponds, nature displays, an aquarium, playground and farm shop.

Kettlewell is an excellent base for walking as the Dales Way passes right through the village, whereas the traffic passes by. Walkers make full use of its guest houses and pubs after days spent exploring the riverside paths, the moors and the minor Dales near by. A popular route is to take a path heading south over Knipe Scar and then head along the River Skirfare and up the lesser-known but delightful Littondale with 2,000-foot (610m) hills on either side of the valley.

KIRKBY LONSDALE
MAP REF SD6178

This tiny market town stands just over the border in Cumbria and marks the far western limit of the Yorkshire Dales. It is a delightfully unspoiled place, whose charms have been recognised by artists and authors, from Constable and Turner to Ruskin and Wordsworth, all of whom have sung its praises over the years.

A Roman fort has been excavated at Burrow, just 2 miles (3.2km) south of the town, and in 1227 King Henry III granted a market charter which allowed for a weekly market and an annual fair to be held in the town. The fair died out in the 19th century, but the market still thrives every Thursday in Market Place. Here the the lovely butter cross is not ancient but dates from the early 20th century. The importance of the old market is shown by the many street names which grew up around it: Market Street, Horse Market, Swine Market.

A street which should be seen is Mill Brow, a steep street of stone buildings which leads down to the river. Down the centre, at one time, ran a stream that not only provided the town's drinking water but was also used to power no less than seven mills.

The Church of St Mary the Virgin is a most impressive building. It is thought to date from the late 11th and early 12th centuries, and a Norman archway beneath the solid square tower is a beautiful construction. It has some fine stained glass and a delicately carved pulpit. Outside, near the north entrance, is a tower which can be seen in J M W Turner's famous painting of 1822, *Kirkby Lonsdale Churchyard*, which serves as another reminder of the timeless nature of this attractive little town, with its charming street names such as Jingling Lane and Salt Pie Lane.

On the edge of town, the medieval Devil's Bridge spans the River Lune. It is one of the town's most notable features with three graceful arches striding over the water and is a very popular meeting place for bikers. Its date is not known for sure, though records from the late 14th century tell of repairs to a bridge in the town. Nor is it known when it first acquired its cheerful name, although a poem of 1821 tells the tale. A Yorkshire woman, known for being a cheat, one night heard her cow and pony calling from the far side of the swollen river. The devil appeared and offered to build a bridge, and his payment would be to keep the first thing that crossed over the bridge. Expecting to receive the cow and pony, he was tricked by the canny

woman who threw a bun across the bridge, which her dog chased after. The devil grinned at the woman's trickery, and disappeared in flames. The bridge is now open for pedestrians only, to help preserve it. A short way down the river is a piece of limestone, known as the Devil's Neck Collar, through which a hole has been worn by the action of the water.

PEN-Y-GHENT   MAP REF SD8373

The lowest but not the least of this region's Three Peaks, Pen-y-ghent in profile seems to be thrusting a jaw out defiantly as if challenging anyone to climb to the top of its 2,277 feet (694m). In its capacity as the third highest of the Three Peaks, many people assume it is the third highest peak in the Yorkshire Dales. This honour, in fact, goes to Buckden Pike, which is 25 feet (8m) higher than Pen-y-ghent. Buckden Pike is 10 miles (16km) across in Wharfedale, though, so even the incredibly fit fell runners would have to think twice about turning the Three Peaks Race into a Four Peaks Race.

Unusually, for this most distinctive of Yorkshire's hills, Pen-y-ghent carries a Celtic name, meaning 'hill of the border', once marking the edge of one of the British tribes' kingdoms. For those who want to tackle its challenge, the most common route is a 3-mile (4.8km) hike from Horton in Ribblesdale, following the signs for the Pennine Way, which passes right over the top of the hill.

At the end of the track out of Horton, just beyond the point where the route turns sharp right towards the hill, there are two potholes. The larger is the huge gaping hole known as Hull Pot, into which Hull Pot Beck disappears. Treat these potholes with extreme caution.

The climb up to the summit of Pen-y-ghent is steep in places, with a little bit of scrambling. At the top, walkers can revel in views across to the other peaks, north across the fells of Langstrothdale Chase, and south over Ribblesdale and Lancashire's Forest of Bowland.

WHERNSIDE MAP REF SD7381

This is the highest point in the Dales, reaching to 2,415 feet (736m). Like Ingleborough and Pen-y-ghent, it owes its existence to the time when, over 300 million years ago, this part of the world wasn't a walker's paradise but a tropical sea. The seabed became thick with the shells of dead creatures, and eventually became the Great Scar Limestone that now lies up to a depth of 600 feet-thick (183m) underneath much of this part of the Dales, its scale most clearly visible at Malham Cove. The Great Scar was mostly buried under sandstones, shales and other limestones deposited by the rivers that drained into the ancient sea. It is these extra deposits, which are known as the Yoredale Series of rocks, which form the tops of the Three Peaks and cover much else in the Dales.

There are a number of approaches to Whernside, but the two most popular are from the Ribblehead Viaduct and Chapel-le-Dale. Maps are needed, but the walks are so busy that the routes are being eroded. Visitors are advised to keep to the official paths, to save further erosion of this dramatic landscape.

■ Activity

THE PENNINE WAY

Britain's first long-distance footpath is the ultimate challenge for many keen walkers. Its 256 miles (412km) from Derbyshire to Scotland includes a 60-mile (97km) stretch in the Yorkshire Dales, entering, as does this book, near Keighley, and leaving past the lonely Tan Hill Inn, where Yorkshire gives way to Durham. One of the walk's main instigators was Tom Stephenson, secretary of the Ramblers' Association at the time, and 2,000 ramblers attended the route's official opening on 24 April 1965 on Malham Moor. Though the route near Pen-y-ghent gives a rugged climb over moors scarred by caves and potholes, there are easier and more low-lying stretches, such as along Airedale, south of Malham, which are all well signposted.

■ Insight

PEREGRINE FALCONS

Watch out in this rugged region for a possible glimpse of peregrine falcons. These beautiful, sleek birds of prey can attain speeds of well over 100mph (160kph) when diving in a 'stoop', falling through the sky with their wings folded back to attack their prey at high speed. Visitors should be aware that it is illegal to approach a peregrine's nest, and a licence is required even to photograph them – should you be lucky enough to see one at close range!

■ Visit

RADICAL STEPS

The Radical Steps, which lead down to the river near Ruskin's View, were built in 1829 by Dr Francis Pearson. They allowed people access to the river, without having to trespass on Dr Pearson's land, which the public footpath crossed before he had it diverted in 1820. The steps gained their name from Dr Pearson's radical views.

■ TOURIST INFORMATION CENTRES

Grassington
National Park Centre,
Colvend, Hebden Road.
Tel: 01756 751690

Horton in Ribblesdale
National Park Information
Point, Pen-y-ghent Café.
Tel: 01729 860333

Ingleton
Community Centre Car Park.
Tel: 015242 41049

■ PARKING

There are pay-and-display
car parks at most of the
National Park Centres, and
visitors are encouraged to
use them. Congestion is a
problem in some villages.

■ PLACES OF INTEREST

Bentham Pottery
Bentham.
Tel: 01524 261567

Ingleborough Cave
Clapham.
Tel: 01524 251242
Tours of cave formations,
streams and lit pools.

Ingleton Waterfalls Trail
The Falls, Ingleton.
Tel: 01524 241930
A 4.5 mile (7.2km) circular
trail on boardwalks in the
gorge and through meadows
and woodland.

Kilnsey Park and Trout Farm
Kilnsey.
Tel: 01756 752150
Visitor centre, fishery,
playground and farm shop.

Parcevall Hall Gardens
Off B625 between
Grassington and Pateley
Bridge.
Tel: 01756 720311

Upper Wharfedale Folk Museum
Grassington Square,
Grassington.
Exhibits relating to Upper
Wharfedale housed in
18th-century lead-miners'
cottages.

White Scar Cave
On B6255 north of Ingleton.
Tel: 01524 241244
Britain's largest show caves,
with tours to falls and rivers.

■ SHOPPING

Grassington
Several shops sell outdoor
clothing, maps, and books
about the area.

Ingleton
Open-air market, Fri.

Kirkby Lonsdale
Open-air market, Thu.

■ LOCAL SPECIALITIES

Crafts
Country Harvest,
A65, Ingleton.
Tel: 01524 242223

Locally Produced Food, Gifts and Crafts.
Curlew Crafts,
Main Street, Ingleton.
Tel: 01524 241608

Pottery, Jewellery, Fossils
Cornerstones, Main Street,
Ingleton. Tel: 01524 242135

Outdoor Clothing and Equipment
Daleswear Ltd,
A65 New Road, Ingleton.
Tel: 01524 241477
Over and Under,
Low Hall, Kettlewell.
Tel: 01756 760871
Pen-y-ghent Café,
Horton in Ribblesdale.
Tel: 01729 860333

Pottery
Ingleton Pottery, Bank
Bottom, Ingleton.
Tel: 01524 241363

Paintings, Prints and Books
The Dales Book Centre, Main
Street, Grassington.
Tel: 01756 753373

■ OUTDOOR ACTIVITIES & SPORTS

ANGLING
Fly
Ingleton: 6 miles (9.7km) of
trout fishing on local rivers.
Permits available from
Village News, Main Street,
Ingleton. Tel: 015242 41683
Kilnsey Park Trout Farm.
Tel: 01756 752150

CAVING & CLIMBING

Horton in Ribblesdale

There are innumerable opportunities for climbing and caving throughout the area. For guided instruction try Yorkshire Dales Guides, Langcliffe.
Tel: 01729 824455; www.yorkshiredalesguides.co.uk

CYCLE HIRE

Kettlewell

W R M Wilkinson,
The Garage.
Tel: 01756 760225

GUIDED WALKS

Contact the National Park Centre, Colvend, Hebden Road, Grassington.
Tel: 01756 751690

HORSE-RIDING

Kilnsey Trekking and Riding Centre, Homestead Farm, Conistone. Trekking and weekly holidays.
Tel: 01756 752861;
www.kilnseyriding.com

LONG-DISTANCE FOOTPATHS & TRAILS

The Dales Way

A fantastic 81-mile (130km) lowland walk through the heart of the Yorkshire Dales connecting Ilkley in the south with Bowness-on-Windermere in the north.

The Ingleborough Estate Nature Trail

A superb trail, which starts at the National Park Centre at Clapham and leads to Ingleborough Cave.

■ EVENTS & CUSTOMS

Burnsall

Burnsall Feast and Fell Race, early Aug.

Clapham

Gaping Gill public descents by winch and bosun's chair each August Bank Holiday week.

Grassington

Grassington Festival, mid-Jun to early Jul.

Horton in Ribblesdale

The Three Peaks Race, end Apr.
Horton Gala and Pen-y-ghent Race, Jun.
Horton in Ribblesdale Show, late Sep.
Ribblehead Sheep Show, late Sep.
Annual Three Peaks Cycle-Cross, late Sep.

Hubberholme

On New Year's Day the 'Hubberholme Parliament' sits in the George Inn after a church service.

Ingleton

Annual Fellsman Hike, Ingleton to Threshfield, early May.
Gala and mountain race, mid-Jul.
Horticultural Show, early Sep.

Kilnsey

Kilnsey Show, late Aug.

RIVER WENNING, CLAPHAM

Tea Rooms

Pen-y-ghent Café
Horton in Ribblesdale, Settle BD234 0HE
Tel: 01729 860333
An institution among walkers, cyclists and runners who take up the Three Peaks Challenge, this is more than just a place for a mug of tea and a piece of home-made cake (though it is excellent for that). The weekend safety service ensures walkers can log in and log out when their day is completed.

West Winds
Buckden, Skipton BD23 5JA
Tel: 01756 760883; www.westwindsinyorkshire.co.uk
Tucked away back behind the village, West Winds is a lovely little hideaway and a real treasure. There is a big log fire to warm yourself by on cold days and a garden for the hotter ones. You might be tempted by the substantial filled Yorkshire puddings, or the home-made cakes – the fruit cake is served with a slice of Wensleydale cheese.

Country Harvest
Ingleton, Carnforth LA6 3PE
Tel: 015242 42223; www.country-harvest.co.uk
On the roadside just north of Ingleton, this is a great place to linger on your way home, or to take stock as you enter the Dales proper. The shop offers locally produced food and crafts. You can sample many of the items, including breads baked fresh on the premises, in the excellent coffee shop.

Town End Farm
Scosthrop, Airton, Skipton BD23 4BE. Tel: 01729 830902
Town End Farm has a lovely tea room and a farm shop filled with tempting goodies. When you've tasted their light snacks – including quiches, sandwiches, baked potatoes – you can stock up on some of the best locally produced food in the area, including Limestone Country grass-fed beef, which is excellent.

Pubs

White Lion
Cray, Skipton BD23 5JB
Tel: 01756 760262; www.whitelioncray.com
Tucked into Cray Gill at the foot of the Kidstones Pass and once used by passing drovers, the White Lion now serves home-cooked food and a range of wine and real ales in the stone-flagged bar. On warmer days it is popular to sit outside, either in the beer garden or by the beck that cascades down in front of the pub.

George Inn
Kirk Gill, Hubberholme, Skipton BD23 5JE
Tel: 01756 760223; www.thegeorge-inn.co.uk
The George was a favourite of writer J B Priestley. The 'Hubberholme Parliament' still sits here at New Year, but year-round it is popular with visitors who come for the locally sourced lamb, pork and beef dishes and the inevitable Black Sheep beers.

King's Head
The Green, Kettlewell, Skipton BD23 5RD
Tel: 01756 760242; www.kingsheadatkettlewell.co.uk
Locally made sausages feature on the menu, which also includes lamb, pork and steak pies. Vegetarians are also catered for and there is a range of cask-conditioned beers to choose from.

New Inn
Clapham, Settle LA2 8HH
Tel: 01524 251203; www.newinn-clapham.co.uk
The New Inn is well known among walkers, cavers and cyclists. The menu, using locally sourced ingredients, has a faintly Mediterranean/Asian twist, but the range of beers are from Lancashire and Yorkshire, and include Copper Dragon ales.

DENTDALE

Wensleydale

If there is one dale above all others that people associate with the Yorkshire Dales, it is Wensleydale. It is the longest, running for over 40 miles (64km), and has some of the prettiest landscapes in the region. Where other dales have rugged features, Wensleydale's are softer and rounded, the slopes of its hills lush and green, its pastures grazed by large flocks of sheep and broken up with long stretches of drystone walls. Its name is also known far and wide because of Wensleydale sheep and Wensleydale cheese.

WENSLEYDALE

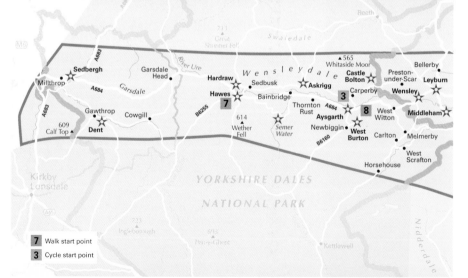

7 Walk start point

3 Cycle start point

WESTBURTON

NEAR ASKRIGG

NORTH YORKSHIRE

Richmond

Catterick

Fencote

Northallerton

East Hauxwell

Patrick Brompton

Leeming Bar

Crakehall

Aiskew

Bedale

Jervaulx

Thornton Watlass

East Witton

River Ure

Burneston

Pickhill

Ellingstring

Snape

High Ellington

Masham

Nosterfield

Healey

West Tanfield

Ainderby Quernhow

North Stainley

Wath

Ripon

Unmissable attractions

Seek out James Herriot's fictional Darrowby in Askrigg...stroll through one of the last remnants of the ancient forest of Wensleydale to Aysgarth Falls or discover the Burton Force waterfall at the beautiful village of West Burton, where time has stood still...explore Castle Bolton, where Mary, Queen of Scots was imprisoned for six months...visit Hawes for good local produce and their busy market on Tuesday... soak up the atmosphere at Jervaulx Abbey, a Cistercian monastery founded in 1156 ...pick up an antique bargain at Leyburn, the largest auction centre outside London... walk around Yorkshire's largest natural lake, Semer Water, ringed by three pretty villages – Countersett, Marsett and Stalling Busk.

1 **Bolton Castle**
Built at the end of the 14th century, this massive edifice dominates the Wensleydale village of Castle Bolton.

2 **Aysgarth Falls**
The River Ure cascades over limestone steps in a series of falls at Aysgarth.

3 **Dent Head Viaduct**
This impressive viaduct carries the Settle–Carlisle Railway line over the valley.

4 **Leyburn Shawl**
The Leyburn Shawl is a very pleasant walk with breathtaking views.

5 **River Ure**
Just one of the many sturdy stone bridges spanning the River Ure.

6 **Jervaulx Abbey**
The atmospheric ruins of a Cistercian monastery, founded in 1156.

ASKRIGG MAP REF SD9491

Though it may only be small, Askrigg demonstrates well the ebbs and flows of history. It received its market charter in 1587, but only because Wensley, sited further down the dale, had been almost wiped out by the plague in 1563. The result of this was the further decline of Wensley and prosperity for Askrigg, where a number of local industries blossomed alongside the busy weekly market: clock-making, brewing, spinning and dyeing.

The age of steam brought a downturn to Askrigg's commercial fortunes, as the Wensleydale railway station was situated at Hawes – less than 3 miles (4.8km) away, but sufficiently distant to ensure the switch to Hawes as the main tourist focus of Wensleydale, which it remains to this day. However, when television location scouts were scouring the area for an unspoiled Dales town to represent Darrowby in James Herriot's veterinary drama, *All Creatures Great and Small*, it was Askrigg that fitted the bill. Now visitors are here again, but to see the locations used for filming, and Askrigg continues to flourish.

AYSGARTH MAP REF SE0088

The Aysgarth Falls are not actually sited in Aysgarth, but just outside the village centre on the road to Carperby. Visitors need not worry about missing them, though, as this is a major Wensleydale attraction and therefore well signposted, with a Yorkshire Dales National Park Centre, adjoining car park and a busy little cluster of shops and cafés catering for the crowds.

The name Aysgarth means an open place marked by oak trees, and as visitors walk through the woods to view the Middle and Lower Falls, few realise that they are strolling through one of the last remnants of the ancient forest of Wensleydale, which once covered most of the countryside here.

There are three sets of falls at Aysgarth – Upper, Middle and Lower – each with their differing attractions, though their appeal lies in the width of the river at this point and visitors must not expect torrents of water tumbling from on high. These falls are gentler, but still extraordinarily beautiful, with the Upper Falls perhaps the best of all. They are on privately owned land and the landowner has introduced a small admission charge, by way of an honesty box, for providing access to the best viewpoints. Some avoid the charge by walking round to view the falls from the road near by and the 18th-century bridge, but the road is both busy and narrow, and its zig-zag curve either side of the bridge reduces visibility. Better to pay just a small charge than to cause a large accident.

Before heading off to look at the rest of the falls, pick up the useful walk leaflet from the National Park Centre, which provides lots of information about the woodlands you'll be walking through and the local wildlife. On the far side of the bridge from the Upper Falls, the signed path leads down to the Middle and Lower Falls. This is a pleasant walk through the leafy woodland known as the Freeholders' Wood, but watch out for the side paths through the trees that lead to views of these other falls, which are narrower but with deeper plunges, the Lower Falls being the most impressive. The path is fairly easy as far as the Middle Falls, but becomes trickier underfoot further on as it begins to step down, so elderly visitors or those with young children are advised to take care. It is about a mile (1.6km) from the Upper down to the Lower Falls.

The Freeholders' Wood through which you pass is now being managed by the National Park Authority, though its freeholders are mainly people from the next village, Carperby, who retain certain rights on the land such as the free gathering of firewood.

Around the bridge and car park there are several gift shops and a tea shop. You can help pay for eventual restoration of the main mill building by paying just 20 pence for the privilege of using the mill's external staircase to give you a superior view of the Upper Falls.

BEDALE MAP REF SE2688

To include Bedale in Wensleydale is stretching a point just a little, as it is in the next valley east of the River Ure, but it is an attractive old market town through which most people will pass if driving from the A1 into Wensleydale. It is worth a stop, though, and a foray into the countryside around.

Bedale gained its market charter in 1251, with a market cross that dates from the 14th century. On the wide main street stands Bedale Hall, a Georgian mansion which today serves as rather grand council offices. Inside is the Tourist Information Point and a tiny local

■ Visit

THE HERRIOT CONNECTION

Carperby is still one of the Dales' quieter villages, with an 18th-century market cross and a 19th-century Quaker Meeting House, though fans of the author and vet James Herriot like to visit to see the Wheatsheaf Hotel, in which he and his wife, Helen, spent their honeymoon in the 1930s.

museum, whose main exhibit here is a fire engine from 1748. The local church contains a 400-year-old bell, which was rescued from Jervaulx Abbey after the Dissolution of the Monasteries.

Bedale also has a station on one of Britain's 'newest' railway lines. The Wensleydale Railway runs from Leeming Bar in the Vale of York to Leyburn and Redmire (for Bolton Castle) in Wensleydale. The original line ran all the way to Garsdale Head to meet with the Settle–Carlisle Railway, but was closed in the 1960s. In 2003 campaigners were able to lease 22 miles (35km) of old track and begin running trains again. Bedale Station reopened in 2004, and is now served by diesel rail car units every couple of hours in the summer months, and at weekends in winter. The latest ambitious plans for the railway include an extension to the East Coast mainline at Northallerton, and a restoration of the Settle–Carlisle link by bringing trains right the way up the dale through Hawes to Garsdale Head.

To the south of Bedale, off the B6268, is the Thorp Perrow Arboretum, which has more than 2,000 species of plants and trees in its 85 acres (34ha) of garden

■ Visit

HIT FOR SIX

The village of Thornton Watlass, 2 miles (3.2km) south of Bedale, is an attractive place, the archetypal English village with a large green on which cricket is played in summer. If visiting the village pub, the Buck Inn, when a match is on, take care not to park in front of the building: the pub wall forms part of the boundary!

and woodland. These in their turn are set in more than 1,000 acres (404ha) of lovely parkland owned by Sir John Ropner, who now manages the fine Arboretum created by Colonel Sir Leonard Ropner over a period of almost 50 years. Many of the species of trees are extremely rare in the British Isles, and some of the oaks on the site are known to date from the time of the Tudors and Henry VIII. It is a beautiful collection at any time of year, but especially during springtime when bluebells, cherry blossom or when the daffodils are in bloom.

CASTLE BOLTON MAP REF SE0391

Castle Bolton is a one-street village that most people pass through on their way to Bolton Castle, which was built in the 14th century. The castle was commissioned by Sir Richard Scrope as an impressive residence rather than for any defensive purposes. Documents covering the construction still survive, and include a licence to crenellate, dated 1379, and a builders' contract from 1378 that refers to the construction of the 'Privees'. The facilities have been modernised since those days!

If you climb to the top of the turrets for the splendid views, try to imagine the vast tracts of Wensleydale Forest that covered the region in medieval times. The Scropes were a Norman family and had been landowners in Yorkshire since the 12th century. Sir Richard was born in 1328, became Member of Parliament for the County of York in 1364 and rose to serve as Chancellor of the Exchequer twice. The castle was completed in 1399 at a cost of £12,000, the equivalent of well over £4.5 million today.

The magnificent four corner towers that rise to 100 feet (30.5m) give only a small indication of the grandeur of the original building. There were eight halls, each acting as independent household units inside the castle.

Bolton Castle's most notable resident, albeit unwillingly, was Mary, Queen of Scots, who was imprisoned here in July 1568 for six months. The bedchamber in which she is thought to have stayed can be seen, and has been decorated in appropriate style, as have many other parts of the castle. Tapestries, arms and armour are on display and tableaux give a vivid impression of life in the castle over the years – including a rather scary dungeon, a hole in the ground into which prisoners were dropped and forgotten about. One arm bone was found down there, still held by an iron manacle.

On the ground floor, just off from the courtyard, are the brew house, the bake house, the meal house, the forge and the threshing floor. On the first floor is the ruined great hall, with the state chamber and guest hall, while up above is a chapel and some monks' cells.

DENT MAP REF SD7086

If there were ever a vote for the most attractive village in the Dales, it would hardly be surprising if Dent won first prize. It is a beautiful cluster of pretty whitewashed cottages and cobbled streets nestling in the lush green valley that is Dentdale. This does, of course, mean that it is extremely busy in the holiday season, and is a place perhaps best visited at other times if possible, when it regains its village charm.

Dent is on the Settle–Carlisle Railway line and is the highest mainline station in Britain, at 1,150 feet (351m), but if you are planning to travel by train, be warned that the station is 5 miles (8km) from the village itself. There is only a connecting bus service on Saturdays (a Wednesday service goes once a day from Cowgill, which is about half a mile/800m down the valley), so visitors need to arrange a lift or a taxi. When one local was asked why they built the station so far from the village, he bluntly replied: "Appen they wanted t'put it near t'track'.

Dent boasts a flourishing artistic community, counting knitters, musicians, authors and photographers among its diverse population. You can see many craft items made for sale in the area. The local Dent Brewery ales are also very popular.

The brewery began in the Sun Inn at the centre of the village but grew so successfully that it had to seek new premises at Cowgill, further up the valley. In Dent there are a number of cafés and pubs and a choice of accommodation and souvenir shops. The Dent Village Heritage Centre, on the western edge of the village, tells the story of the valley, its people, industry and wildlife.

Adam Sedgwick was born in Dent in the Old Parsonage in 1785, attended the local grammar school and then went on to become Woodwardian Professor of Geology at Cambridge. He retained his connection with Dent, and the pink Shap granite memorial fountain in the main street marks his distinguished career as a geologist. This was not always merely a memorial, as it also provided the town's main water supply until the 1920s. In 1985, to commemorate the 200th anniversary of his birth, the National Park Authority created the Adam Sedgwick Geology Trail, near Sedbergh. Leaflets are available at National Park Centres and Tourist Information Centres.

Near by the Sedgwick Stone, you'll find St Andrew's Church, which has a Norman doorway, although most of the church was actually rebuilt in the late 19th century. Inside are some unusual Jacobean box-pews and flooring of Dent marble. Both black and grey marble were quarried near here in the past. The Stone House Marble Works flourished in the 18th and 19th centuries at Arten Gill, southeast of Dent Station, where you will also find the Dent Head Viaduct, yet another of the marvellous constructions on the Settle–Carlisle Railway line. Many of the line's stations contain marble that was quarried at Dent. In the days when the quarries were working, the knitters were busy knitting and the mills were humming with weaving, Dentdale's population reached almost 2,000 – about three times what it is today.

HARDRAW FORCE

HARDRAW MAP REF SD8792

Hardraw is a hamlet that would probably be visited only by those passing through on the Pennine Way if it was not for the existence of Hardraw Force. At 96 feet (29m) it has the longest free drop of any waterfall in England – above ground, at least – and was painted by Turner on his travels through the Yorkshire Dales. Another unusual feature is that to reach it you must pass through the Green Dragon pub, paying a small entrance fee as you do so. The volume of water from the fall is not great, and it is therefore best visited after heavy rain. Those who do not mind a slight splashing can walk round behind the fall, although care must be taken on the wet rocks as they are slippery. In 1739 and 1881, the falls froze completely to produce an impressive 100-foot (30.5m) icicle.

The Force falls into a pool in a natural amphitheatre, and the acoustics here are such that an annual brass band contest takes place every September, a tradition that goes back to 1885. Past winners include famous names such as the Black Dyke Mills Band and Besses o' the Barn. The contests once included choirs who stood on the ground above the Force and sang with the bands, but this was not a raging success as they were unable to hear each other. The contests died out for a time but have been revived and are once more a great attraction.

HAWES MAP REF SD8789

Family businesses make up the shops in the main street in Hawes, and it is certainly the place to stock up on good local produce, especially on the busy Tuesday market day when stalls line the streets and farmers conduct their business at the livestock market along the Leyburn road – which visitors, too, should take a look at, for a flavour of farming life in the Dales.

To sample Wensleydale cheese, and the chance to watch it being made, head for the Wensleydale Creamery. This factory, built in 1897 by a local corn merchant, has a visitor centre, which includes a museum, video display, licensed restaurant, shop, free cheese-tasting and viewing platforms into the works. The best time to see Wensleydale being made is 10.30am to 3pm.

A more conventional museum is the fascinating Dales Countryside Museum, in the Station Yard. The arrival of a railway link in 1877 boosted Hawes' fortunes, as the town had only received its market charter in 1700 after Askrigg, and previously Wensley, had been the focal points of Wensleydale. The trains no longer run but Hawes is now well established as the main town of Upper Wensleydale. The museum (which also contains a Tourist Information Centre and a National Park Centre) has first-class displays on life in the Dales, particularly on small local industries such as knitting and peat-cutting. Its collection is enhanced by the inclusion of Yorkshire Dales material donated by the local authors and historians, Marie Hartley and Joan Ingilby. Just across from the Station Yard is the entrance to Outhwaite and Son, rope-makers, where visitors can see how the rope is produced as well as buy rope products, gardening items and gifts in the shop.

Visit

THE TURNER TRAIL

J M W Turner visited Wensleydale and Swaledale in 1816, and produced a great number of paintings as a result of his trips. At 16 of the sites he painted, or is known to have visited, seats have been erected to enable visitors to enjoy the same stirring views. A leaflet from Tourist Information Centres entitled 'The Turner Trail' lists these places.

Activity

TAKE THE HIGH ROAD

Drive south out of Hawes through Gayle, heading for Kettlewell, and you will cross Wether Fell and Fleet Moss Pass, reaching a height of 1,857 feet (566m). This is the highest road in the Yorkshire Dales, and one of the highest in all England.

Visit

COLSTERDALE

To the west of Masham is one of the least-known Dales, the lonely Colsterdale, with a road that leads to some peace and fine views. It is a fitting place for a memorial to the Yorkshire regiment known as the Leeds Pals, who were massacred in July 1916 during the Battle of the Somme.

JERVAULX MAP REF SE1786

This superb Cistercian monastery, now mostly in ruins, is a truly evocative place, filled in summer with the scent of the glorious wild flowers that grow around the crumbling grey stones. The abbey was founded in 1156 and eventually owned much of Wensleydale. Sheep, cattle and horses were bred by the monks, who were the first to make Wensleydale cheese.

Despite the fact that the buildings are in a ruinous state there is still plenty to see, such as the staircase, known as the Night Stairs, which led the from the monks upstairs dormitory to night services in the church. Other abbey remains that can be identified include the cloister, the infirmary, the kitchen and the parlour. It is unfortunate but the abbey was destroyed with particular ferocity when King Henry VIII began his Dissolution of the Monasteries in 1536. The last Abbot of Jervaulx, Adam Sedbar, or Sedbergh, was a vociferous opponent of the Dissolution and his protests caused him to be hanged at Tyburn Hill in London. Jervaulx is on private land but open access is allowed to visitors, with an honesty box for admission money. There is a car park, a very pleasant tea room and souvenir shop.

LEYBURN MAP REF SE1190

Leyburn is yet another of the towns in the Yorkshire Dales that has staked a claim to being the unofficial capital of Wensleydale. It flourished when plague affected the village of Wensley in 1563, though the all-important market charter was granted to Askrigg, and Leyburn did not receive its charter until 1684. The Friday market flourishes in the market square. A modern addition is a purpose-built auction centre on Harmby Road, the largest outside London, which holds general and specialist sales two or three times a month.

Close by is a ceramics workshop where you will find the Teapottery, an unusual if not unique establishment which makes and displays nothing but teapots. You can watch the craftspeople at work, making pots in every shape and size – the only thing they do not make are teapots that look like teapots.

There are many other craft shops in Leyburn, which are scattered in-between mainly 19th-century town houses. On the western edge of the town, beginning in Shawl Terrace not far from the Tourist Information Centre, is the walk around the area known as the Leyburn Shawl. This easy stroll to an open grassy area is a popular with locals and visitors alike, as it leads very quickly to some glorious views of Wensleydale.

MASHAM MAP REF SE2280

Visitors to Masham (pronounced by the locals as 'Massam') are welcomed by its cobbled Market Place, one of the largest in the country and providing ample car parking in the centre of the town. It is an indication that Masham was once much more important than it appears today, a pleasant but less bustling town than many, though you are guaranteed a busy day. Masham's position was its making, between Wensleydale's sheep-filled hills and the flatter crop-growing fields of the Vale of York. It's also within easy reach of both Fountains Abbey to the south, and Jervaulx Abbey to the north. In those days its large Market Place was much needed, not merely for its weekly market but also its annual Sheep Fair, both of which date back to 1250.

Standing off one corner of the Market Place stands the old parish church of St Mary, whose rather strange-looking tower came about in the 15th century when a bell-stage and a tall spire were

■ Insight

THE MASHAM SHEEP FAIR

The origins of this fair go back to 1250, when it was granted by charter. It was so successful that as many as 70,000 sheep would be exhibited and sold, but the show died out after the First World War with the spread of road and rail transport, and the ease of taking sheep direct to the larger auctions, rather than drive them to Masham. The event was revived in 1986, however, when a local woman, Susan Cunliffe-Lister, decided that Sheep Aid could be added to events like Live Aid and Fashion Aid as a means of raising money to help alleviate the African famines. The Sheep Fair flourished once again, and still does, with rare and prize sheep on display, sheepdog demonstrations, crafts and many other visitor attractions.

added to the original Norman base. The church was mentioned in the Domesday Book and its oldest feature is a carved stone Anglo-Saxon cross, which dates from the early ninth century. There is some dispute as to what these now rather weathered carvings were first meant to represent.

Noted for its craft shops, Masham's heritage also rests in its fine brewing industry, with two breweries open for inspection. The longer established of these is Theakston's. The brewery has a visitor centre and the chance to see some of the country's few remaining coopers at work, building their barrels. Brewery guided tours must be booked well in advance. The same applies to the Black Sheep Brewery, so called because it belongs to a renegade member of the Theakston family.

Hawes and Hardraw

These two popular settlements both have something to offer visitors and walkers – Hawes is famous for Wensleydale cheese and motorcyclists, who congregate here on summer weekends, and Hardraw for its spectacular waterfall. The walk in-between takes in farmland and moorland scenery. Despite appearances, what you see at the Hardraw Falls isn't entirely natural. On 12 July 1889 an unprecedented deluge on the hill above caused a wall of water to descend Hardraw Beck and through the valley, destroying buildings in the villages and washing away bridges. The local landowner, Lord Wharncliffe, seeing the devastation to the villagers – his tenants – then arranged for his workmen to reconstruct the lip of the fall.

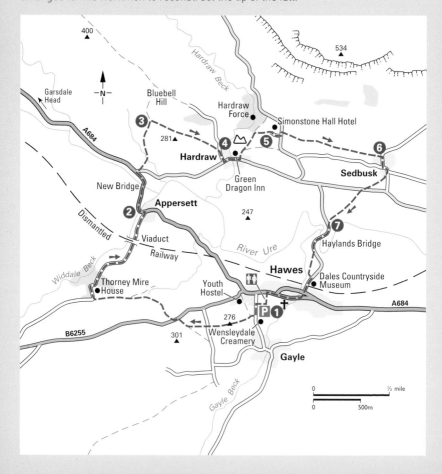

Route Directions

1 From the car park turn left. Just before the Creamery turn right between houses. Follow the left side of the field to a stile at the top. Keep straight on past a barn and across a lane. After passing a ruined barn, bear right to the B6255. Turn left, then right through a gate signed 'Thorney Mire House'. Follow the path, which bears left between parallel walls, for 0.5 mile (800m) to meet a lane. Turn right and follow this to the A684 at Appersett.

2 Turn left over the bridge. Continue over another bridge to a junction, turn right and go straight over a stile, signed 'Bluebell Hill'. Bear slightly right to a gate and over a bridge, then bear left uphill to reach a gate. Continue past waymarks to a signpost.

3 Turn right and walk to a stile (Bob's Stile) then bear slightly right to a prominent ladder stile. Walk straight ahead and Hardraw soon appears. Continue down over a stile, then over a ladder stile into a lane.

4 Turn right, then left at the main road. Hardraw Force entrance is through the Green Dragon pub. Immediately after the pub, turn left, then

right through a signed gap in the wall and through a courtyard. Follow a flagged path and steps uphill to a house. Turn right behind it, pass right of the stables, then bear slightly left to pass below the grounds of Simonstone Hall Hotel, joining its drive.

5 Walk down to a road and turn left. Almost immediately turn right through a stile signed 'Sedbusk'. Follow the track past farm buildings to a ladder stile, then continue straight ahead. Skirt below a house and continue over more stiles, along a flagged path and between houses into Sedbusk.

6 Turn right along the road, bend left near the postbox and descend. Go right, over a stile signed 'Haylands Bridge'. Cross the field, bear right below a wall-corner to a stile, then descend to a stile by the right end of a line of trees. Cross the lane to another stile and follow an obvious path across a stream. Descend to a humpback bridge and continue to a road.

7 Turn left and cross Haylands Bridge. About 200yds (183m) beyond, go right through a kissing gate signed 'Hawes'. Follow the

path to a track, turn left a few paces, then right on to the main road. At the junction, cross the first road, then turn right past the post office. Follow the main road through Hawes. Immediately before the public toilets, turn left up steps to the car park.

Route facts

DISTANCE/TIME 5 miles (8km) 2h

MAP OS Explorer OL30 Yorkshire Dales – Northern & Central

START Pay car park off Gayle Lane at west side of Hawes, grid ref: SD 870898

TRACKS Field and moorland paths, may be muddy, 35 stiles

GETTING TO THE START
Hawes is on the main A684 road, which links the M6 near Sedbergh with the A1 near Northallerton. This bustling market town has two car parks. The one used here is at the west side of the town, just off the minor road to Gayle.

THE PUB Green Dragon Inn, Hardraw. Tel: 01969 667392; www.greendragonhardraw. co.uk

❶ Take care on the bustling Hawes streets

Green Ways of Wensleydale

This route follows a magical green ribbon of a bridleway along a broad terrace high above the valley.

Route Directions

1 Cross the footbridge and follow a tarmac path out to a wider, roughly surfaced lane. Bear right, up to a road and turn right. After 2 miles (3.2km) Carperby is a left turn signed for Castle Bolton, and the main climb of the route. Pass close under the corner of one of the towers and at the top turn left, following signs for the car park and toilets.

2 Where the lane swings up into the car park, keep ahead through a gate and along an easy track. Follow the track through several gates and skirt to the left of some large wooden farm sheds; there can be muddy splashes here. After passing through the next gate, the track becomes a little rougher, wiggling left through another gate and then right again. The track beyond is distinctly rougher, especially where it dips at a small ford; many may prefer to dismount and walk here.

3 At the next gate bear left above the wall, on easy grassy going with some wheel ruts and a few avoidable rocky patches. After some

almost lawn-like grass, dip to a ford, sometimes dry but still quite rough. More good grassy going follows. At the next gate bear half left on to a smooth green track, following signposts to Askrigg and Carperby, which gives delightful and easy riding for the next 0.5 mile (800m) to reach Low Gate.

4 At Low Gate keep ahead up the hill on more smooth green track, signed for Askrigg. Level out and descend to a gate where a rougher track (Peatmoor Lane) crosses. Follow the green track ahead, across a level grassy plateau, until it descends to Oxclose Gate. From here the track skirts left of conspicuous bare ground and the spoil heaps on the site of a former lead mine.

5 Opposite this area the track acquires a good gritty surface, and soon swings down to a gate, with a ford just beyond. Dismount and wheel the bikes across this ford and beware of the drop just below. Next, follow the stony track through another gate. Beyond this gate a short section is

Route facts

DISTANCE/TIME 9.75 miles (15.7km) 1h30; extension 12.5 miles (20.1km) 2h

MAP OS Explorer OL30 Yorkshire Dales – Northern & Central

START Small car park on A684, Aysgarth, grid ref: SD 995889

TRACKS Grassy tracks; a few short rough sections; return on lanes, muddy after rain

GETTING TO THE START Aysgarth is on A684 road through Wensleydale. Park by footbridge 0.5 mile (800m) west of the village.

THE PUB The Wheatsheaf Hotel, Carperby. Tel: 01969 663216; www.wheatsheafin wensleydale.co.uk

❶ Steep climb on road, short sections of rough track, steep descent. Longer loop only suitable for older, experienced children. Mountain bikes essential.

sometimes wet but can be avoided by skirting to the right, crossing ruined walls. Go up to another gate, swing left through it and down 50yds (45.7m) to a signpost.

6 For the shorter of the two loops, descend the steep, twisting track to Woodhall. The surface is loose in places, and inexperienced riders should dismount and walk

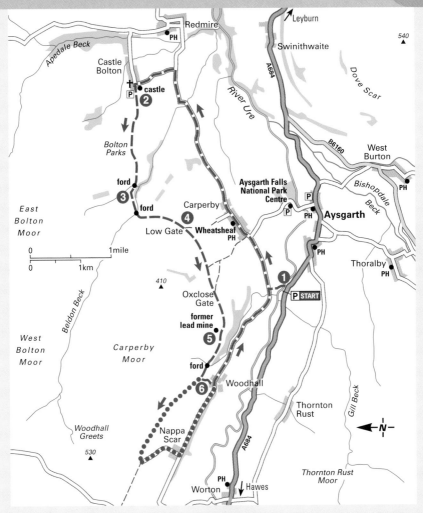

down. Turn left on the wider road for an easy run, almost entirely downhill, back to the start. For the extension , turn right and then climb the steep rough track. After two gates the gradient eases and the track winds through some hummocks. Go through a gate

alongside a small plantation. Beyond is the final climb, very tricky in places with bare rock and large loose stones; only experts will ride it all. Over the top there's smooth grass, then a final section of rutted track leads to a gate by a barn. The track beyond

soon begins to descend, getting steeper and rougher. At a junction turn sharp left, almost immediately meeting tarmac. Follow the steep lane, which can have an overlay of loose grit in places, down into the hamlet of Nappa Scar and turn left on to the wider road.

MIDDLEHAM   MAP REF SE1287

Middleham's claim to be the smallest town in Yorkshire is not the least of its distinctions, as it also has two market places and a collection of horse-racing stables that have seen it referred to as the 'Newmarket of the north'. It has certainly produced its share of race winners over the years, and of course the racecourses of Thirsk, Ripon, Wetherby and York are all near by. Anyone staying in Middleham will wake up to the clip-clop of hooves on cobbles as the stable lads and lasses take the horses up to the gallops on the moors above the town for an early-morning workout.

The most important landmark in the town is its fine Norman castle (cared for by English Heritage), which is in a very good state of preservation. Some of the remains date back to 1170, although there was another castle in Middleham prior to that. The castle was put on the map by Richard III, who first came to Middleham in 1461 when he was Duke of Gloucester. His tutor in riding and other skills was the Earl of Warwick, and Richard married his daughter, Anne, in

1472. They stayed at Middleham after marriage – their son, Edward, was born in the castle – and lived here until Richard, became king in 1483, when he was required to leave for London. By 1485 he was dead, killed in the Battle of Bosworth Field, and Middleham never resumed its royal importance.

Richard also would have attended Middleham's church, St Alkelda's, much of which dates back to the 13th and 14th centuries. From the lower market place are splendid views down the dale, and with plenty of pubs, tea shops, gift shops, accommodation and eating places, Middleham shows that it may be a small town but it has much to offer.

SEDBERGH   MAP REF SD6591

Thanks to the quirks of local government boundary changes, the largest town in the Yorkshire Dales National Park is actually in Cumbria. Even so, Sedbergh's population is still under 3,000 and it has an eye-catching setting. To the north are the high Howgill Fells; to the south the green fields fall away, across the River Rawthey to the River Dee, which runs through Dentdale. Sedbergh, a popular centre, is just 5 miles (8km) east from junction 37 of the M6 and is the main western gateway to the Yorkshire Dales. The Tourist Information Centre on Main Street is where you'll find interpretative displays, maps, walks, guides and local information for visitors who intend to stride out and enjoy the beauty of the Yorkshire Dales. It also has information about Sedbergh's 'Book Town' status, and its various fascinating book and literary events.

◼ Visit

FARFIELD MILL

On the edge of town, down by the River Clough, Farfield Mill is a restored early Victorian textile mill. As well as Dobcross looms producing fine quality fabrics, there is an art and craft gallery, a textile heritage museum, a pottery, woodworkers, a café, shop and woodland walks. The mill is run by a trust which is seeking to restore substantial links between farming and industry in rural life.

The Normans gave Sedbergh its parish church and a motte and bailey castle. Little remains of the castle save a few grassy mounds and the name of the road leading to it, Castleshaw, but the Church of St Andrew is worth seeing, with its ancient pews and alms boxes. Close by is the minuscule Market Place, where a market has been held for almost 750 years. The Market Cross was removed in 1897 when Finkle Street was widened and other alterations made to the town as part of Queen Victoria's Diamond Jubilee celebrations. The top of the cross now stands in the garden of the Quaker Meeting House in Brigflatts, a tiny village, which lies just over 1 mile (1.6km) southwest of Sedbergh off the Kirkby Lonsdale road. The village was once an industrial community and the Meeting House, built in 1675, can still be visited. It is the oldest in the north of England and retains many of its original furnishings. It has been described by many writers as one of the most peaceful places anyone could imagine.

Sedbergh School was founded in 1525 by a local man called Roger Lupton, who went on to become Canon of Windsor and Provost of Eton. Lupton founded the school for 'theym of Sedber, Dent, and Garstall', although today it is one of the best-known public schools in Britain. A new school was built in 1716, which is now used as a museum and library, and the buildings in use today date mainly from the late 19th century.

It is the old buildings of Sedbergh that are its main attraction. Much of the Main Street has been designated a Conservation Area. As well as narrow alleys and tucked-away yards, Main Street contains many fine dwellings. Webster's Chemist's Shop dates from the first half of the 17th century, and behind it is Weaver's Yard, where the first weaving looms in Sedbergh were set up. From here, just at the back of Webster's, a 17th-century chimney breast can be seen – one of the many places around Britain in which Bonnie Prince Charlie is said to have hidden at one time or another. Some of Sedbergh's other delights are hidden, too, so be sure to make time to wander the streets and enjoy this delightful little town.

SEMER WATER MAP REF SD9187

Yorkshire's largest natural lake was formed in Raydale during the ice age when a retreating glacier left behind a huge clay dam, and another was blocked in by a glacier in Wensleydale. The resultant melt water formed Semer Water, which is now a very popular place busy with anglers, boaters, watersports enthusiasts, nature lovers, swimmers, walkers and those who simply want to stop and admire the splendid views.

It's possible to walk all the way round the lake, which is ringed by three pretty little villages – Countersett, Marsett and Stalling Busk – with a fourth settlement said to be lying on the bed of the lake! Another explanation for the lake's origins claims that a beautiful city once stood here. An angel, disguised as a beggar, went round the city appealing for food and drink, but was turned away at every home. The angel left the city and finally found food and shelter in the home of a poor man and his wife. On leaving the next morning, the angel turned to the city and said:

'Semerwater rise – Semerwater sink,
And cover all save this lile house
that gave me meat and drink.'

The waters did indeed rise to create the lake, and beneath its surface you may just hear the occasional sound of bells ringing from the long-drowned city. The poor man's cottage survived, and is said to be at Low Blean, on the eastern edge of Semer Water.

WENSLEY MAP REF SE0989

Wensley is one of the small villages that many people pass through on their way to the attractions of the dale that took the village's name. It is hard to imagine that this was once the main settlement in Wensleydale, being the first place to receive a market charter, as long ago as 1202, with the only market in the whole of the dale for the following 100 years. Wensley flourished until plague struck the village in 1563, when the focus of Wensleydale life shifted a mile (1.6km) to the east, to Leyburn, and later westward to Askrigg and then Hawes.

Church of the Holy Trinity is a reminder of that importance, with parts of the building dating from 1240. Its pale stone tower was built in 1719, and inside you will find an 18th-century pulpit and a 17th-century font. There's also a memorial to the Scrope family, from Castle Bolton, near by, who had close connections with the church. When the Scropes built Bolton Hall in 1678 Wensley began its regrowth as an estate village.

Near the church is the gate that leads to Bolton Hall, and also near here is the river on which there is a small waterfall and Wensley Mill. Today this houses the White Rose Candle Workshop. Visitors can watch the process of candle-making, and naturally there is a shop where you can purchase candles.

WEST BURTON MAP REF SE0186

This beautiful village is just off Wensleydale, at the point where Walden Beck flows out of Waldendale and into Bishopdale, giving West Burton a delightful waterfall, Burton Force, just a short stroll from the village centre. Below the fall is a packhorse bridge, which adds to the charm of the scene. At West Burton's centre is one of the largest village greens in the country, a great expanse like a grassy lake, its sloping sides lined by old stone cottages with tree-covered hills rising up behind them. Many of the cottages were built for workers in the quarrying and lead-mining industries. The main road, such as it is, bypasses the village centre leaving it as an almost timeless place, where children can play and horses can graze and visitors can feel they have stepped back at least 50 years in time. Situated on the heart of the green is a cross, which was put up in 1820 and rebuilt in 1889. It is believed that the stone cross replaced a more ancient marker, as at one time this was the location for a weekly market which catered for the needs of a much larger population. On one side of the green is a pub, on the other the Cat Pottery, which specialises in life-like ceramic cats.

From West Burton to Aysgarth

A walk from West Burton to Aysgarth, two typical Dales villages, and back, via the famous Aysgarth Falls on the River Ure and some unusual farm buildings. Many people regard West Burton as the prettiest village in the Dales.

Route Directions

1 Leave the Green near the village shop. Opposite 'Meadowcroft' go left, signed 'Eshington Bridge'. Cross the road, turn right, then left through a gate and down steps. Go through a gate beside a barn and continue to a stile at the bottom right of the field. Cross two more stiles, then bear right to meet a stone wall. Follow this then continue in the same direction to a road.

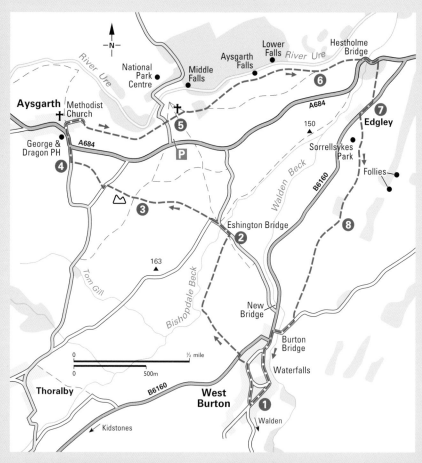

2 Turn left, cross the bridge and go up a narrow lane to a bend. Go ahead through a stile, signed 'Aysgarth'. Climb past another stile and left of a barn. Continue up the field and bear left to a gate near the corner, then diagonally across the next field. Keep left of an obvious wall-gap to a stile by another gap. Descend to a stile and footpath sign.

3 Continue in the same direction and up to a signpost. Follow the Aysgarth direction to a gateway and stile. Cross the field half left to a stile onto a lane. Turn left, then right, signed 'Aysgarth'. Go through three stiles to a road.

4 Turn right, into the village. Go past the George and Dragon then straight ahead to the Methodist Church and bear right along the lane. Cross a stile by Field House. Follow the wall and continue along a short track, then follow a path through eight stiles to a road.

5 Enter the churchyard, pass right of the church and leave by a stile. Cross a field and go through a wood. Follow the path downhill, descending steps to the river bank. Take a signed stile right.

6 Follow the path by the river to a signpost. Bend right across a field to the main road. Turn left, cross a bridge, then turn right into woodland, signed 'Edgley', soon bearing left, uphill, to a stile. Bear right across a field to a gate in the far corner and join a road.

7 Turn right. About 150yds (137m) along, go left over a stile, signed 'Flanders Hall'. Walk towards the follies, then bear right just below the ridge, passing Sorrelsykes Park to your right. Cross a track and bear left past a waymark to a signpost. Turn right to a stepped stone stile, then follow the bottom edge of the field to reach a gate opposite a stone barn.

8 Descend through this and two more gates, then bear left along the field edge to a stile. Continue ahead to a lane. Turn right, cross a bridge and join the village road. Turn left, back to the Green.

Route facts

DISTANCE/TIME 4 miles (6.4km) 1h30

MAP OS Explorer OL30 Yorkshire Dales – Northern & Central

START Centre of West Burton, by (but not on) the Green, grid ref: SE 017867

TRACKS Field and riverside paths and tracks, 35 stiles

GETTING TO THE START West Burton lies at the convergence of Bishopdale and the Walden Valley. It's a mile south of the A684 Wensleydale road and can be accessed by taking the B6160 between West Witton and Aysgarth. There's no car park but there's plenty of space around the village green.

THE PUB The George & Dragon, Aysgarth. Tel: 01969 663358; www.georgeanddragon aysgarth.co.uk

❶ The main road at Aysgarth can be very busy at the weekend.

■ TOURIST INFORMATION CENTRES

Bedale
Bedale Hall.
Tel: 01677 424604

Leyburn
4 Central Chambers, Railway
Street. Tel: 01748 828747

Sedbergh
Main Street.
Tel: 01539 620125

■ PARKING

Pay-and-display car parks in
most National Park Centres.

■ PLACES OF INTEREST

Bedale Hall
Bedale.
Tel: 01677 423797

**Black Sheep Brewery
Visitor Centre**
Masham.
Tel: 01765 680100

Bolton Castle
Castle Bolton.
Tel: 01969 623981

Dales Countryside Museum
Station Yard, Hawes.
Tel: 01969 666210

Dent Village Heritage Centre
Dent. Tel: 01539 625800;
www.dentvillageheritage
centre.co.uk.

Jervaulx Abbey
Open access.

Middleham Castle
Middleham. Two miles
(3.2km) south of Leyburn
on the A6108 road.
Tel: 01969 623899

**Theakston Brewery Visitor
Centre**
The Brewery, Masham.
Tel: 01765 680000;
www.theakstons.co.uk

Thorp Perrow Arboretum
Bedale.
Tel: 01677 425323

**Wensleydale Creamery
Visitor Centre**
Gayle Lane, Hawes.
Tel: 01969 667664

Wensleydale Railway
Leeming Bar Station.
Tel: 0845 450 5474

White Rose Candles
Wensley Mill, Wensley, near
Leyburn. Tel: 01969 623544
Free.

■ FOR CHILDREN

**The Big Sheep
& Little Cow Farm**
Aiskew Watermill,
Aiskew, Bedale.
Tel: 01677 422125 Tour
of farm and animals.

Holme Farm
Sedbergh. Off A683.
Tel: 01539 620654
Working farm by river.

■ SHOPPING

Bedale
Open-air market, Tue.

Hawes
Open-air livestock and street
market, Tue.

Leyburn
Open-air livestock and
produce market, Fri.

Masham
Open-air market, Wed.

Sedbergh
Open-air market, Wed.

■ LOCAL SPECIALITIES

CHEESE & HONEY
Apart from the Wensleydale
Creamery in Hawes, many
shops stock Wensleydale,
Coverdale and other local
cheeses, and local honey.

CRAFTS
The Cart House, Hardraw.
Tel: 01969 667691
Craft items, gifts, tea room.

Glass
Uredale Glass, Masham
Studios, Market Place,
Masham.
Tel: 01765 689780
Glass-blowing
demonstrations.

Ice-cream
Brymor Ice-Cream,
near Jervaulx.
Tel: 01677 460377
Award-winning ice cream
from pedigree Jersey cows.

Jewellery
The Rock and Gem Shop,
off Market Place, Hawes.
Tel: 01969 667092

Pottery
The Cat Pottery, Moorside
Design, West Burton.
Tel: 01969 663273
The Gallery, 24 Market
Place, Masham.
Tel: 01765 689554

Pottery and Handmade Jewellery

The Teapottery,
Harmby Road, Leyburn.
Tel: 01969 623839

Prints & Artwork

Focus on Felt, Hardraw.
Tel: 01969 667644
Wensleydale Galleries,
Leyburn Business Park,
Harmby Road, Leyburn.
Tel: 01969 623488

Rope

Outhwaite and Son, Town
Foot, Hawes.
Tel: 01969 667487. See rope
being made in workshops.

Wool Products

Wensleydale Longwool
Sheepshop, Cross Lanes
Farm, Gariston, Leyburn.
Tel: 01969 623840
Sophie's Wild Woollens,
The Shop on the Green,
Vicarage Lane, Dent.
Tel: 01539 625323

■ OUTDOOR ACTIVITIES & SPORTS

ANGLING

Fly

Masham: Leighton Reservoir.
Four miles (6.4km) southwest
of Masham; day tickets on
sale in the car park.
Sedbergh: Parts of Lune and
Rawthey, also Clough and
Dee. Permits available from
Three Peaks Ltd,
25 Main Street.
Tel: 015396 20446

Fly & Coarse

River Ure permits available
from The Coverbridge Inn,
Coverbridge.
Tel: 01969 623250

CYCLE HIRE

Hawes

Kudu Bikes, Upper
Wensleydale Business Park.
Tel: 01969 666088;
www.kudubikes.co.uk

GUIDED WALKS

Contact the Tourist
Information Centres or
National Park Centres.

HORSE-RIDING

Bainbridge

Wensleydale Equestrian
Centre.
Tel: 01969 650367

Masham

Swinton Riding and Trekking
Centre, Home Farm, Swinton.
Tel: 01765 689241

LONG-DISTANCE FOOTPATHS & TRAILS

The Herriot Way

A 56-mile (90km) circular
route from Aysgarth through
the National Park following
an itinerary associated with
James Herriot.

■ EVENTS & CUSTOMS

Dent

Dent Gala, late Aug.

Hardraw

Hardraw Brass Band
Festival, contact The Green
Dragon, Hardraw.
Tel: 01969 667392

Hawes

Hawes Gala, late Jun.

Jervaulx

Jervaulx Horse Trials,
early Jun.

Leyburn

Wensleydale Agricultural
Show, Leyburn, late Aug.

Masham

Masham Steam Engine and
Fair Organ Rally, Jul.
Masham Sheep Fair, Sep.

Middleham

Open days in racing stables.
Contact Leyburn Tourist
Information Centre for dates.
Middleham Festival, Jun.

Semer Water

Outdoor church service on
Sun of August Bank Holiday
weekend.

West Witton

The West Witton Feast and
the Burning of Bartle, Sat
nearest to 24 Aug.

Tea Rooms

Stone Close Tea Room
Main Street, Dent,
Sedbergh LA10 5QL
Tel: 01539 625231
The whitewashed Stone Close has built a well-earned reputation for serving wholesome food, including for vegans and vegetarians. Molly cake is a particular favourite – dates and fruit without sugar, fat, gluten or dairy. The lunch menu might include aduki bean casserole or lamb hotpot.

Bordar House
13 The Market Place,
Masham HG4 4DZ
Tel: 01765 689118
Sit in Masham's huge market square and enjoy a delicious afternoon tea with Yorkshire teacakes or home-made fruitcake and Wensleydale cheese. This is a proper old-fashioned tea shop where light lunches of omelette and chips, or toasted sandwiches are the order of the day. A blackboard has daily specials.

Jervaulx Abbey Tea Rooms
Jervaulx, Ripon HG4 4PH
Tel: 01677 460391;
www.jervaulxabbey.com
Just across the road from the abbey ruins, the Abbey Tea Rooms do swift trade with visitors using the car park. Sit outside in the garden and enjoy the delicious home-made honeycakes, or scones, or sit inside for something more substantial.

The Coppice Coffee Shop
Aysgarth Falls National Park Centre, Aysgarth, Leyburn DL8 3TH. Tel: 01969 663763
The Coppice has long been a welcome sight to visitors to Aysgarth Falls. Right next to the National Park Centre and the car park and bus stop, it's an ideal place for a light lunch – the filled jacket potatoes are popular. Locally sourced ingredients are used whenever possible.

Pubs

Sun Inn
Main Street, Dent, Sedbergh LA10 5QL. Tel: 01539 625208
Dent may feel like a village in which time has stopped still, but the Sun Inn was a true pioneer in the revolution that revitalised many country pubs. The Dent brewery was established behind the pub in 1990, and though it has since moved up the road to larger premises, you can still enjoy its excellent output here, particularly when suitably accompanied by no-nonsense food – the tasty sausages and pies are truly excellent.

The Blue Lion
East Witton,
Leyburn DL8 4SN
Tel: 01969 624273;
www.thebluelion.co.uk
The stone-flagged floors and real fire setting don't detract from the thoroughly modern approach to food where chargrilled fillet of local beef might be served with a Shiraz sauce, shallots, lardons and mushrooms. Local Masham beers in the bar.

Green Dragon Inn
Hardraw, Hawes DL8 3LZ
Tel: 01969 667392; www.greendragonhardraw.co.uk
Even without the access to Hardraw Force behind the pub, you would still want to visit the Green Dragon for its hand-pulled ales and traditional food including game casserole and home-made steak pie.

Rose and Crown Hotel
Bainbridge, Leyburn DL8 3EE. Tel: 01969 650225;
www.theprideofwensleydale.co.uk
This large inn with three bars and a restaurant serves a good mix of wines, Masham beers, and food from a menu that ranges from toasted goats cheese salad or Cumberland sausage and mash to seafood cannelloni.

Swaledale & the North

INTRODUCTION

Swaledale is the grandest of all the dales, its rugged dramatic beauty is more appealing to some than the prettier and busier Wensleydale. It is a dale of fast-flowing streams and waterfalls, of a string of small villages with harsh-sounding Norse names such as Keld and Muker. At its eastern end stands Richmond, a busy and civilised market town, with a castle and no less than three museums. At its western end, visitors and walkers will feel as if they have left civilisation far behind as the road climbs and curves through some fantastic scenery towards Mallerstang. Both are dales of tremendous character.

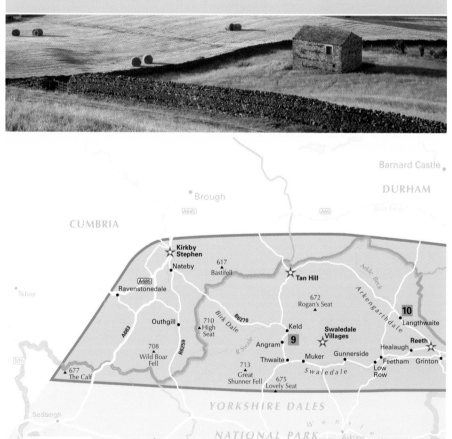

9 Walk start point

VIEW OVER MUKER

CELTIC SIGN, ANGRAM

Unmissable attractions

Explore Swaledale, the most peaceful and least developed of the great valleys – once a centre for lead mining and hand knitting...discover the smart town of Richmond with its great castle high on the hill standing guard over the entrance to the dale and its large cobbled market place, where the River Swale spills out into the lowlands of the Plain of York...visit the remote and attractive villages of Reeth, Keld and Muker... experience the breathtaking contrasts of light and dark, between the meadows and the brooding hills...chance upon the impressive parish church of Kirkby Stephen.

1 Kirkby Stephen
Known locally as the 'Cathedral of the Dales', the fine parish church of Kirkby Stephen contains many ancient relics.

2 Muker
One of the attractive Swaledale villages, Muker, a cluster of squat stone cottages, is approached over a sturdy bridge.

3 Gunnerside
Meadows, divided by drystone walls and dotted with barns, surround the village of Gunnerside. Up on the fells are the remains of the lead-mining industry.

4 Richmond Castle
Richmond's castle stands in ruins on a rocky promontory above the River Swale. It was built by Earl Alan Rufus shortly after the Norman invasion.

5 Swaledale
Stone barns, part of an older farming pattern, form one of the most important visual aspects of the Dales. They were built to store hay after it was cut, to feed the a few animals that would be over-wintered inside.

KIRKBY STEPHEN

MAP REF NY7708

If this unspoiled town started to market itself as yet another 'Gateway to the Dales', no one could complain at the description for although it is in Cumbria, it stands at the foot of Mallerstang, a dale which stretches south, half-in and half-out of the Yorkshire Dales National Park. While Kirkby Stephen tends to get lost between the Yorkshire Dales and the Lake District, the inhabitants know exactly where they stand, referring to their parish church as the 'Cathedral of the Dales', an apt description for a magnificent church.

While the rest of Kirkby Stephen may not quite live up to its impressive parish church, it is still an enjoyable place to linger, with several guest houses and welcoming pubs, though fewer souvenir shops than you might expect. Many people might think that this is all to the good. The town does attract a large number of visitors as it is on the famous Wainwright Coast-to-Coast Walk.

■ Insight

NORSE NAMES

The Norse word for a woodland clearing was 'thwaite' or 'thveit', and other common Norse endings are 'sett' and 'side', which tend to occur in the north of the Dales: Appersett, Gunnerside, Swinithwaite. The 'sett' ending derives from *saetr*, which describes the Norse practice of driving their animals to the higher pastures for summer grazing. The typical isolated Dales barn is another result of this way of living. Norse words include many that are still used today, such as fell, beck, gill and force.

The parish church is certainly one of the region's hidden gems, containing many fine features. There are some well-preserved bread shelves, a fine Shap granite and Italian marble pulpit, and a 17th-century font. A beautiful engraved panel over the entrance to the Hartley Chapel shows the Stoning of St Stephen; it was made by John Hutton, who was also responsible for the memorable glass screen in Coventry Cathedral. Inside the chapel is a tub once used to measure a bushel of wheat. The remains of a 13th-century piscina, a basin with a drain where water used in ceremonial occasions is poured away, can also be seen.

The finest of all the church's features is the Loki Stone, a 10th-century Anglo-Danish cross carved with the features of the Norse God, Loki. The stone is the only such example in Britain, and one of only two in the whole of Europe. The oldest part of the present church dates from 1220. Prior to that, this was the site of a Norman church which only survived for 50 years, and before that a Saxon church is known to have stood on this spot. Exploring the churchyard reveals a flat stone table. This is the Trupp Stone, on which the tenants of church properties would traditionally pay their tithes. It was in use until 1836. Also of historical interest are the attractive cloisters at the entrance to the church grounds, where once the butter market took place. In sunlight the stone is an appealing buttery colour.

About 4 miles (6.4km) south of Kirkby Stephen, by the side of the B6259, stand the atmospheric remains of Pendragon

Castle. In truth there is more atmosphere and myth than historical fact here, for even though the castle is named after King Uther Pendragon, the legendary father of King Arthur, the building actually only dates from the 12th century. The castle is crumbling and not very big, and although on private land there is open access for the public.

REETH MAP REF SE0399

Tucked quietly away in the junction where Arkengarthdale meets Swaledale, Reeth appears much larger and more important than the other Swaledale villages. This is due to the huge green, surrounded by 18th-century houses, that dominates the place, and the sprawling nature of the village itself. Today Reeth is an attractive centre for tourism, with general shops, craft shops, pubs, a few hotels and guest houses, and the dale's most important museum.

The Swaledale Folk Museum, which also acts as an information centre for visitors, is hidden away behind the post office on the far eastern side of the Green. Inside there are particularly good displays on the dale's main industries over the years: farming and lead-mining. The latter is long-gone, and there was money to be made from the former, as information about a local farmer's sale of a ram for £30,000 indicates.

Reeth received its market charter in 1695, and although there is still a market on Fridays, it is a small affair compared to most places. Of more interest to visitors these days are the several craft shops that are supported by Reeth's main business today: tourism.

About 3 miles (4.8km) west of Reeth, on the minor road that goes north from Feetham, is Surrender Bridge. Over the bridge on the right is a track that takes you to the remains of the Surrender Lead Smelting Mill, now a scheduled Ancient Monument. There were extensive lead workings in this area. The industry dates from Roman times but it was at its peak in the 18th century.

RICHMOND MAP REF NZ1701

To approach Richmond from Swaledale is to see the importance of the town to the dale. The road winds through lovely wooded valleys, eventually revealing Richmond Castle standing on its hill high above the river. The castle, now cared for by English Heritage, dates from the Norman period and inside is Scolland's Hall, which dates from the 11th century and claims to be the oldest hall in England. The panoramic views down the river and over the surrounding area are splendid.

Behind the castle is Richmond's huge cobbled Market Place, with its Market Cross and the unusual sight of Holy Trinity Church: unusual because there are shops and a museum built into the base of the building, which was almost destroyed several times and then later restored, since its construction in around 1150. The curfew bell sounds from the church's clock tower, at 8am and 8pm every day. It's also known as the 'Prentice Bell', because as well as sounding the curfew, it marked the start and end of the apprentices' working day. At one time, the town crier, who lived beneath the bell was responsible, for ringing it each day.

A convenient rope meant that the morning bell could be rung without him having to get out of bed.

The museum in the church is that of the Green Howards, one of Yorkshire's proudest regiments. Inside are smart modern displays, which the historian or military buff will find fascinating, but this is actually only one of three museums in Richmond. The Richmondshire Museum itself is a typical collection of historical items, from prehistoric to the age of television and James Herriot.

■ Visit

THE 'CORPSE WAY' TO GRINTON
The parish church of St Andrew in Grinton was for centuries the church for the whole of Swaledale. People who died in the upper reaches of the Dale would have to be brought to Grinton on what became known as the 'Corpse Way'. There are a number of Norman remains at the church, although most of it dates from the 13th to 15th centuries. Note the hole in the wall known as the Leper's Squint, which allowed afflicted people to observe the service at a safe distance from the rest of the congregation.

■ Visit

POOR OLD HORSE
The 'Poor Old Horse' is a mummer's play performed in and around Richmond in the week before Christmas and up to New Year's Eve. During the play the horse dies, but rises again in a reflection of its traditional pagan role as a bringer of good luck and fertility. Poor Old Horse is accompanied by red-coated attendants, redolent of the Richmond Hunt, and can traditionally be found in the town centre on Christmas Eve.

When the BBC finished filming the first series of *All Creatures Great and Small*, not knowing that when screened it would go on to become one of the most popular series ever made, they sold the set for James Herriot's surgery to the museum. With a second series on the horizon, the BBC asked if they could buy it back, but the museum, sensing by then that it had an exhibit of great interest to visitors, refused. The BBC was forced to build a replacement. No doubt James Herriot would have recognised these as canny Yorkshire business dealings.

Richmond's best museum, however, is the Georgian Theatre Museum. The theatre, built late in the 18th century, is the only one in the world that still survives in its original state. As well as attending a show in the evenings, visitors should take one of the guided tours to have a glimpse behind the stage, into the dressing rooms and inside the original box office. Volunteer guides make the place come alive.

A mile (1.6km) southeast of the town centre, via a walk along the banks of the Swale, is Easby Abbey (English Heritage). The ruins of this medieval monastery are impressive, if not quite as grand as the more celebrated Fountains Abbey further south. They certainly make a fitting destination for a pleasant walk, though, where Swaledale comes to an end.

SWALEDALE VILLAGES
Swaledale names are mostly short and sharp, from their Norse origins: Muker, Keld, Thwaite, Reeth, Angram. Even the longer ones are spat out with those

same short Norse vowels: Gunnerside, Arkengarthdale. Most of the villages in this area are short and sharp too, strung out along the B6270 like knots in a rope, but they welcome tourists and offer lots of places to shop, to stay and eat, and a range of local craft studios. Beyond Keld, the 'knots' end, and the lonely road crosses the fells to Nateby and Kirkby Stephen at the northern end of the valley of Mallerstang, as it opens out into the lovely Vale of Eden.

Travelling from Reeth, Gunnerside is the first sizeable community you reach. It is an appealing place with grey stone cottages, which were once the homes of lead miners, looking down on the River Swale with high-rising moors. Norse settlers were attracted by its sheltered location at the confluence of Gunnerside Gill and the larger river. Later on, lead mining brought prosperity to the area, and the remains of several mines can be found just a short distance from the centre of the village. Another walk is to the unusual Ivelet Bridge.

Beyond Ivelet is Muker, a collection of stone cottages clustered in jigsaw streets that zigzag steeply up from the main road. Plaques on the church wall commemorate Richard (1862–1928) and Cherry (1871–1940) Kearton, brothers who were born in Thwaite and went to school in Muker. They devoted their lives to watching wildlife and became early pioneers of wildlife photography. There is also a Literary Institute, an echo of the Norse origins of its unusual name, for Muker meaning 'a cultivated plot'.

Scarcely a mile (1.6km) west of Muker is Thwaite, where the cottage in which the Kearton brothers were born still stands. This idyllic place hides the tragedy of the fearsome flood of 1899 when the waters of Thwaite Beck swept down from Stock Dale in the west and almost wiped out the entire community. It is said that flowers washed from Thwaite's cottage gardens were later found growing in Muker.

The last Swaledale village is Keld, quietly going about its business, set back from the main road in a dead end that leads down to the River Swale and some of Swaledale's most impressive falls. The Pennine Way passes the edge of Keld before heading northwards up Stonesdale to the lonely outpost that is Tan Hill. The Swaledale road goes west through some of the most dramatic scenery in the whole of the Yorkshire Dales before arriving at Nateby, just outside the boundary of the National Park, in the valley of Mallerstang.

TAN HILL MAP REF NY8907

The lonely Tan Hill Inn is the highest pub in England at 1,732 feet (528m), reached via a hairpin road from Keld, 4 miles (6.4km) to the south. It makes the tiny hamlet of Keld look like a city's bright lights. Tan Hill is on the County Durham boundary – in fact boundary changes in 1974 moved the inn from Yorkshire into Durham, but after loyal Yorkshiremen objected to losing their celebrated pub, the boundary was redrawn to the north.

There is no public transport to the pub, so if you wish to visit this isolated spot it will have to be on foot, bike or by car, and preferably during opening hours – so check before you set off.

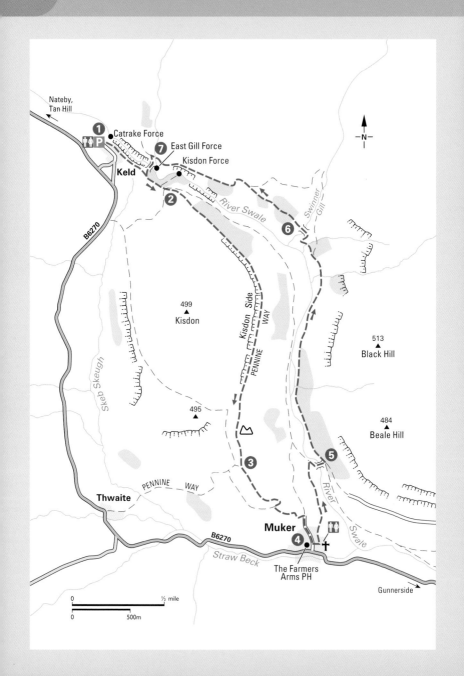

From Keld to Muker

This is a classic walk in Upper Swaledale from Keld to Muker along Kisdon Side and backed by the River Swale. Keld – its name is the Old Norse word for a spring – is one of the most remote of the Dales villages. Set at the head of Swaledale, its small cluster of grey stone cottages is a centre for some of the most spectacular walks in North Yorkshire. It is worth taking some time to explore the village of Muker when you get there. Like many of the Swaledale settlements, it rapidly expanded during the 18th and 19th centuries because of the local lead-mining industry.

Route facts

DISTANCE/TIME 6 miles (9.7km) 2h30

MAP Explorer OL30 Yorkshire Dales – Northern & Central

START Signed car park at west end of Keld near Park Lodge, grid ref: NY 892012

TRACKS Field and riverside paths and tracks, 5 stiles

GETTING TO THE START Keld is set high on pastured hills, right at the end of Swaledale, on the B6270. It is 9 miles (14.5km) from Kirkby Stephen and 20 miles (32km) from Richmond. There is a good car park at the west end of the village.

THE PUB The Farmers Arms, Muker. Tel: 01748 886297; www.farmersarmsmuker.co.uk

Route Directions

1 Walk back down the car park entrance road, and straight ahead down a gravel track, signed 'Muker'. Continue along at the upper level, ignoring a path downhill to the left. Go through a gate, pass a sign to Kisdon Upper Force, and continue along the path below crags to reach a signpost.

2 Turn right, following the Pennine Way, and go up to a gap in a wall and another signpost. Go left and follow a rough but mostly level path along Kisdon Side, first above woodland then across more open slopes. Cross a ladder stile as the path starts to descend. Go down to a signpost and bear right to another signpost, where the Pennine Way goes right.

3 Bear left down a walled track, marked 'Muker'. The track becomes gravelled and then metalled, finally descending into a walled lane on the edge of the village. Continue to a T-junction.

4 Turn left and in a few paces left again by a sign to Gunnerside and Keld. Follow the paved path through six gates to the river. Turn sharp right and walk downstream to a footbridge.

5 Ascend steps beyond the footbridge and turn left, signed 'Keld'. Follow a clear track up along the valley, until it curves right into Swinner Gill. Cross a footbridge by the remains of lead workings, and go up to a wooden gate.

6 Go straight ahead up the hill and through woodland. The track levels out, then starts to descend, winding left round a barn then swinging back right. Continue steadily downhill to reach a gate above East Gill Force.

7 Fork left by a wooden seat, at a sign to Keld. Follow the path down to a footbridge then bear right, uphill, to a T-junction, where you turn right and follow the track back to the car.

Langthwaite in Arkengarthdale

Discover an austere valley where lead workers once toiled leaving a mine-scarred moorland landscape with evocative remains of industry. Arkengarthdale runs north from Swaledale into dark moorland, with battle-scarred Stainmore beyond its head.

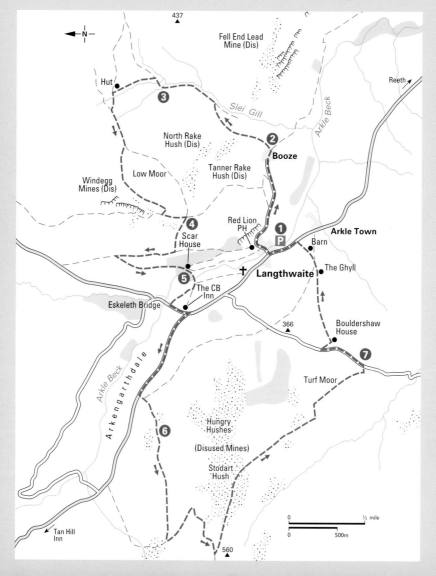

Route Directions

1 Leave the car park, turn right, then right over the bridge into Langthwaite. Climb the narrow lane between cottages. The lane becomes a track. Ignore two left forks and continue to the hamlet of Booze. Go straight through the yard of Town Farm and follow a rutted track up and left to a gate.

2 Continue ahead on a green track slanting down through spoil heaps and past ruined Sleigill House to the stream. Walk up the valley, go through a gate and cross the stream near a limekiln.

3 Climb the steep bank, go through new tree-plantings and follow green paths through the heather. Pass a wooden hut and turn left on a broad track. Follow the main track through a slight valley, then bearing left over the moor and down to a T-junction with a wall just below. Where this falls back, go down right to a gate in the corner.

4 Follow the small gully downhill and past waymarks to a level track. Turn right and follow the track, traversing the hillside until it bends sharp left to meet a stony track. Turn left to a house then bear right, through the garden and down a slanting green track, eventually entering woodland.

5 Emerge alongside Scar House. Follow the drive downhill and over a bridge. Bear right on a walled track, then turn right through gateposts and walk to a road. Turn left, uphill, to a T-junction. Turn right and follow the road for 0.5 mile (800m). Opposite a barn, turn left on an obvious track.

6 Turn right at the far side of a gravelled area, cross a grassy area and slant uphill towards a prominent flat-topped spoil heap. Just before this, the track bends sharp left then winds uphill to reach a T-junction near the crest. Turn left and follow the clear track, along the ridge then bearing right down to a road.

7 Turn left. Pass above a farm (Bouldershaw), then turn right at a bridleway sign. Turn left just before the farmyard and go straight down a green track. At The Ghyll, join its access track but as it bends right bear left and down to a stile in the bottom right corner of the field. Go down to the road. Turn left back to the car park.

Route facts

DISTANCE/TIME 8 miles (12.9km) 3h15

Shorter alternative route: 4.5 miles (7.2km) 2h

MAP OS Explorer OL30 Yorkshire Dales – Northern & Central

START Pay-and-display car park in Langthwaite, grid ref: NZ 005024

TRACKS Mostly clear tracks, some heather moor, 4 stiles

GETTING TO THE START
To reach Langthwaite, follow the A6108 westwards from Richmond, then the B6270 as far as Reeth. From the top of the village green, take the narrow lane signposted to 'Arkengarthdale'. The car park is on the south side of Langthwaite village.

THE PUB The CB Inn, Arkengarthdale.
Tel: 01748 884567;
www.cbinn.co.uk

❶ Full walk is too long for young children – you can shorten the route at Point 5. Navigation would be difficult in mist and low cloud.

■ TOURIST INFORMATION CENTRES

Kirkby Stephen
Market Square.
Tel: 01768 371199

Richmond
Friary Gardens,
Victoria Road.
Tel: 01748 828742

■ PARKING

Pay-and-display parking is available throughout the district with limited free disc parking in Richmond. The parking discs can normally be obtained at Tourist Information Centres, shops, banks and the like.

■ PLACES OF INTEREST

Easby Abbey
Richmond. Medieval abbey remains (English Heritage) set beside the River Swale. Open access to site. Free.

Georgian Theatre Royal
Victoria Road, Richmond.
Tel: 01748 823710; www.georgiantheatreroyal.co.uk
Dating from 1788, the theatre closed down in 1848, but was restored and re-opened in 1962. The theatre is still used for live productions (music, comedy, drama etc) and it has a museum with old playbills, photographs and the oldest complete set of painted scenery in England.

Green Howards Regimental Museum
Trinity Church Square,
Market Place, Richmond.
Tel: 01748 826561
The military history of the Green Howards, going back to the 17th century, is illustrated here, together with displays of uniforms, weapons and medals.

Richmond Castle
Richmond.
Tel: 01748 822493.
Occupying a stunning position overlooking the River Swale, the castle is now in ruins, but visitors can see the keep, two of the towers and Scolland's Hall.

Richmondshire Museum
Ryder's Wynd, Richmond.
Tel: 01748 825611.
Museum of local history.

Swaledale Folk Museum
off the Green, Reeth.
Tel: 01748 884118.
An excellent museum that llustrates the history of the area.

■ FOR CHILDREN

Hazel Brow Farm
Low Row.
Tel: 01748 886224
A 200-acre (80ha) working farm where you can interact with the livestock, discover nature trails and watch the demonstrations of sheep shearing and other events.

■ SHOPPING

Kirkby Stephen
There are antiques shops in Market Street. Open-air market, Mon.

Reeth
Open-air market, Fri.

Richmond
Open-air market Sat. Indoor market Tue, Thu, Fri & Sat.

■ LOCAL SPECIALITIES

Craft Workshop
Reeth Dales Centre, Silver Street, Reeth.
Tel: 01748 884555
A collection of fascinating craft workshops including Philip Bastow, cabinet maker.

Pottery & Damson Cheese
The Garden House,
The Smithy, Anvil Square, Reeth.
Tel: 01748 884188

Sculptures & Portraits
Joy Bently, East Windy Hall,
Arkengarthdale Road, Reeth.
Tel: 01748 884316
Stef's, Reeth Dales Centre,
Silver Street, Reeth.
Tel: 01748 884498
Animal sculptures and models, handmade and hand-painted.

Woollens
Swaledale Woollens,
Strawbeck, Muker.
Tel: 01748 886251
Knitwear hand-crafted from wool from local Swaledale and Wensleydale sheep.

■ PERFORMING ARTS

Georgian Theatre Royal,
Victoria Road, Richmond.
Tel: 01748 823710/823021;
www.georgiantheatreroyal.
co.uk

■ OUTDOOR ACTIVITIES & SPORTS

ANGLING

Fly & Coarse

Day tickets for the River
Swale from Keld to around
Grinton Bridge are available
from the Bridge Inn, Grinton.
Tel: 01748 884224
and from the Post Office in
Reeth. Water levels can be
unreliable in summer so seek
local advice first.

CYCLE HIRE

Richmond

Dales Mountain Biking, Parks
Barn, Fremington.
Tel: 01748 884908; www.
dalesmountainbiking.co.uk

GUIDED WALKS

For information about guided
walks in the area, contact the
local Tourist Information
Centres.

HORSE-RIDING

Reeth

Arklemoor Riding Centre,
East Intake House,
Arkengarthdale Road.
Tel: 01748 884731;
www.arklemoor.co.uk

■ EVENTS & CUSTOMS

Muker

Muker Show, early Sep.

Reeth

Reeth Show, late Aug.

Richmond

The Richmond Meet, Spring
Bank Holiday weekend.
The 'Poor Old Horse'
Mummers' Play takes place
around Christmas.

Swaledale

The Swaledale Festival, late
May to early Jun.

Tea Rooms

Muker Village Store and Tea Shop
Muker, Richmond DL11 6QG
Tel: 01748 886409
This cosy teashop is a part of the Dales landscape. The store looks after the needs of the local community as well as stocking a good range of local produce, while the tea shop has a tempting menu of home-made snacks and cakes. On the Pennine Way, there is bed-and-breakfast accommodation available, too.

Hazel Brow Farm
Low Row, Richmond DL11 6NE. Tel: 01748 886224;
www.hazelbrow.co.uk
With tray bakes, fresh scones, carrot cake and perhaps a 'Hazelbrowman's lunch', the Organic Café at Hazel Brow strives very hard to ensure as much of its produce as possible is certified organic. An imaginative specials board keeps the savoury options fresh and you can buy produce in the farm's shop.

Rattan and Rush
39–41 Market Street, Kirkby Stephen CA17 4QN
Tel: 01768 372123
This is a unique place to drop in for a cup of coffee and a scone on the High Street in Kirkby Stephen. Surrounded by antiques, and a creditable range of folk music CDs, there is a faintly boho feel to the place, which may inspire you to return for one of the excellent folk gigs held here in the evenings.

Ghyllfoot Tearoom
Lodge House, Gunnerside, Richmond DL11 6LA
Tel: 01748 886239
Home-baking and local specialities mark out this delightful teashop in the centre of Gunnerside. There's a terrace and garden at the back facing out on to fields towards Gunnerside Gill, or you can eat inside.

Pubs

Tan Hill Inn
Tan Hill, Richmond DL11 6ED. Tel: 01833 628246;
www.tanhillinn.co.uk
Famous for being the highest pub in Britain at 1,732 feet (528m) above sea level, the Tan Hill stands on truly wild moorland, literally miles from anywhere. Inside though the welcome is as warm as the open fires, and the array of bar food is designed to satisfy the hunger of passing Pennine Way walkers. Good ale and a series of weekend music and motoring events means you'll seldom be short of good company.

The CB Inn
Arkengarthdale, Richmond DL11 6EN
Tel: 01748 884567;
www.cbinn.co.uk
The CB prides itself on fine food and accommodation. Consequently, it attracts a discerning clientele, drawn by tasty fresh fish, including line-caught wild sea bass (delivered every day from Hartlepool), or fillet of beef on an oxtail terrine. The wine list is supported by Black Sheep beers from Masham.

Farmers Arms
Muker, Richmond DL11 6QG
Tel: 01748 886297
The Farmers Arms serves robust steak pie, venison casserole, and even Cumberland sausage and Yorkshire pudding to walkers on the Pennine Way or Coast to Coast. Real ales come from Masham and local microbreweries.

King's Arms
Reeth, Richmond, DL11 6SY
Tel: 01748 884259;
www.thekingsarms.com
All the food at the King's Arms is locally sourced and usually manages to put an interesting twist on standard menu items. Cask-marque ales often include Timothy Taylor's and Black Sheep.

■ NATIONAL PARK CENTRES

AYSGARTH
Aysgarth Falls.
Tel: 01969 662910

GRASSINGTON
Hebden Road.
Tel: 01756 751690
Information screens provide a 24-hour service.

Park Information Points
Kettlewell Village Store; Over and Under, Kettlewell; Riverside Gallery, Buckden; Pen-y-ghent Café, Horton in Ribblesdale; Ingleton YHA; Kettlewell, YHA; Katie's Kiosk on the Green, Burnsall.

HAWES
Dales Countryside Museum, Station Road.
Tel: 01969 666210

Park Information Points
Stone Close Tearoom, Dent; Withywood Stores, West Witton; Grinton Lodge YHA; Hawes YHA; Thoralby Post Office.

MALHAM
Tel: 01969 652380
(There is a 24-hour information screen.)

Park Information Points
Beck Hall, Malham; Cavendish Shop, Bolton Abbey; Bolton Abbey Village Shop; Embsay and Bolton Abbey Railway, Bolton Abbey Station; Malham YHA; Settle TIC; Stump Cross Caverns.

REETH
Hudson House, Reeth.
Tel: 01748 884059

Park Information Points
Hazel Brow Visitor Centre, Low Row; Muker Village Store; Grinton Lodge YHA

■ USEFUL CONTACT INFORMATION

British Waterways Board Yorkshire Office
Fearn's Wharf, Neptune Street, Leeds.
Tel: 0113 281 6860;
www.waterscape.com.

English Heritage
37 Tanner Row, York.
Tel: 01904 601901;
www.english-heritage.org.uk

Environment Agency
21 Park Square South, Leeds.
Tel: 08708 506506; www.environment-agency.gov.uk

National Trust
Yorkshire Regional Office
Goddards, 27 Tadcaster Road, Dringhouses, York.
Tel: 01904 702021;
www.nationaltrust.org.uk

RSPB
www.rspb.org.uk

Yorkshire Dales National Park Authority
www.yorkshiredales.org.uk

Yorkshire Tourist Board
www.yorkshire.com

Yorkshire Wildlife Trust
1 St George's Place, York.
Tel: 01904 659570;
www.ywt.org.uk

■ ORDNANCE SURVEY MAPS

SOUTHERN DALES
Landranger 1:50,000;
Sheets 119, 128.
Explorer 1:25,000; Sheet OL24.

ILKLEY & THE SOUTH
Landranger 1:50,000;
Sheets 104.
Explorer 1:25,000;
Sheet OL21, 297, 288.

GATEWAY TO THE DALES
Landranger 1:50,000;
Sheets 98, 103, 104.
Explorer 1:25,000;
Sheet OL10.

HARROGATE & RIPON
Landranger 1:50,000;
Sheets 99, 104.
Explorer 1:25,000;
Sheets 289, 297, 298.

CENTRAL DALES
Landranger 1:50,000;
Sheets 97, 98.
Explorer 1:25,000;
Sheets OL2, OL30.

WENSLEYDALE
Landranger 1:50,000;
Sheets 98, 99.
Explorer 1:25,000;
Sheets 302, OL2, OL19, OL30.

SWALEDALE & the NORTH
Landranger 1:50,000;
Sheets 92, 98.
Explorer 1:25,000;
Sheet 304, OL19, OL30.

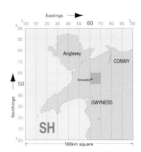

The National Grid system covers Great Britain with an imaginary network of grid squares. Each is 100km square in area and is given a unique alphabetic reference, as shown in the diagram above.

These squares are sub-divided into one hundred 10km squares, identified by vertical lines (eastings) and horizontal lines (northings). The reference for the square a feature is located within is made by adding the numbers of the two lines which cross in the bottom left corner of that square to the alphabetic reference (ignoring the small figures). The easting is quoted first. For example, SH6050.

For a 2-figure reference, the zeros are omitted, giving just SH65. In this book, we use 4-figure references, which allow us to pinpoint the feature more accurately by dividing the 10km square into one hundred 1km squares. These squares are not actually printed on the road atlas but are estimated by eye. The same process is carried out as before, giving an enhanced reference of SH6154.

Key to Atlas

M4	Motorway with number	Toll	Toll	Abbey, cathedral or priory	NTS — National Trust for Scotland property
S Fleet	Motorway service area	Road underconstruction	Road underconstruction	Aquarium	Nature reserve
	Motorway toll	Narrow Primary route with passing places	Narrow Primary route with passing places	Castle	Other place of interest
	Motorway junction with and without number	Steep gradient	Steep gradient	Cave	P•R — Park and Ride location
	Restricted motorway junctions	Railway station and level crossing	Railway station and level crossing	Country park	Picnic site
	Motorway and junction under construction	Tourist railway	Tourist railway	County cricket ground	Steam centre
A3	Primary route single/dual carriageway	National trail	National trail	Farm or animal centre	Ski slope natural
BATH	Primary route destinations	Forest drive	Forest drive	Garden	Ski slope artifical
	Roundabout	Heritage coast	Heritage coast	Golf course	Tourist Information Centre
5	Distance in miles between symbols	Ferry route	Ferry route	Historic house	Viewpoint
A1123	Other A Road single/dual carriageway	6	Walk start point	Horse racing	Visitor or heritage centre
B2070	B road single/dual carriageway	1	Cycle start point	Motor racing	
	Unclassified road single/dual carriageway	3	Tour start point	Museum	Zoological or wildlife collection
	Road tunnel			Airport	Forest Park
				Heliport	National Park (England & Wales)
				Windmill	
				NT — National Trust property	National Scenic Area (Scotland)

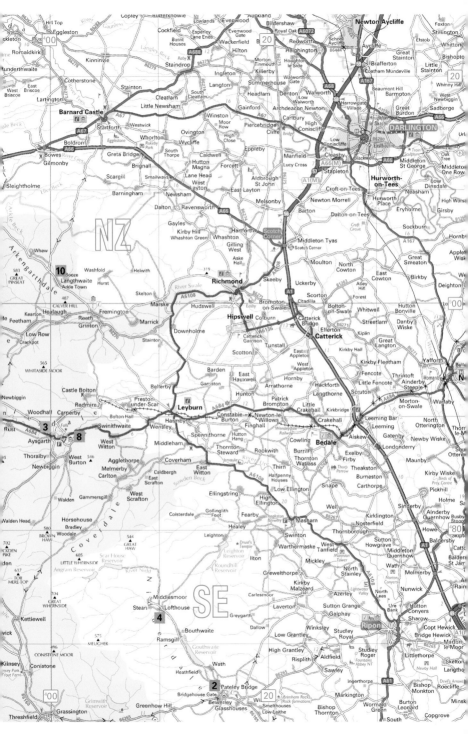

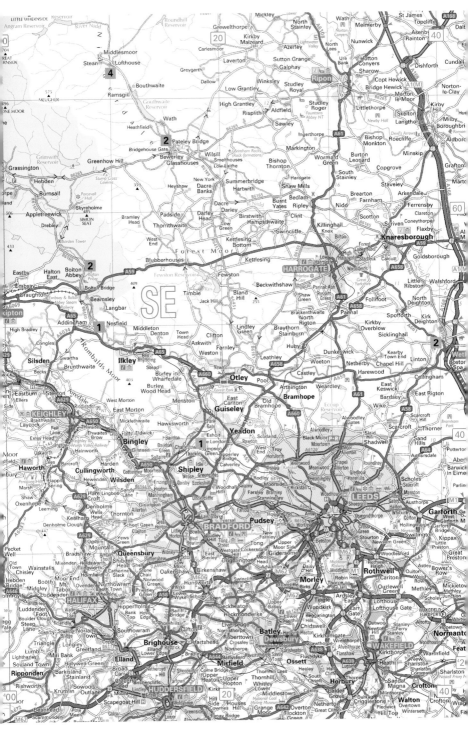

The Automobile Association would like to thank the following photographers and companies for their assistance in the preparation of this book. Abbreviations for the picture credits are as follows – (t) top; (b) bottom; (c) centre; (l) left; (r) right; (AA) AA World Travel Library

1 AA/J Tims; 4/5 AA/H Williams; 8tl AA/L Whitwam; 8cl AA/T Mackie; 8bl AA/T Mackie; 8r AA/S & O Mathews; 9 AA/T Mackie; 10t AA/T Mackie; 10c AA/T Mackie; 10b AA/S & O Mathews; 11t AA/T Mackie; 11b AA/T Mackie; 13 AA/D Tarn; 14tl AA/T Mackie; 14tr AA/P Baker; 14b AA/T Mackie; 18/19 AA/J Tims; 21t AA/P Wilson; 21b AA/D Tarn; 22 AA/T Mackie; 23t AA/D Tarn; 23b AA/T Mackie; 34 AA/D Tarn; 36/37 AA/T Mackie; 39tl J Sparks/Alamy; 39tr AA/T Mackie; 39b AA/T Mackie; 40 AA/D Tarn; 41t AA/T Mackie; 41c AA/T Mackie; 41b AA/T Mackie; 43 AA/T Mackie; 52 S Singh/Alamy; 56 AA/T Mackie; 58/59 AA/T Mackie; 61tl AA/D Tarn; 61tr AA/T Mackie; 61b AA/T Mackie; 62cl AA/ T Mackie; 62cr AA/T Mackie; 62b AA/T Mackie; 63t AA/L Whitwam; 63c AA/T Mackie; 63b AA/W Voysey; 69 AA/T Mackie; 80 AA/D Tarn; 82/83 AA/T Mackie; 85 AA/D Tarn; 86t AA/D Tarn; 86b AA/D Tarn; 87t AA/T Mackie 87c AA/A Baker; 87b AA/T Mackie; 92/3 AA/T Mackie; 98 AA/T Mackie; 104 AA/A Baker; 106/107 AA/T Mackie; 108 AA/T Mackie; 109l AA/T Mackie; 109tr AA/T Mackie; 109br AA/T Mackie; 110l AA/J Morrison; 110r AA/T Mackie; 110b AA/D Tarn; 111t AA/D Tarn; 111c AA/T Mackie; 111b AA/L Whitwam; 116 AA/T Mackie; 127 AA/T Mackie; 132 AA/T Mackie; 134/135 AA/T Mackie; 136 AA/T Mackie; 137t AA/T Mackie; 137b AA/T Mackie; 138tl AA/D Tarn; 138tr AA/T Mackie; 138b AA/D Tarn; 139t AA/P Baker; 139b AA/T Mackie; 150 A Novelli/Alamy.

Every effort has been made to trace the copyright holders, and we apologise in advance for any accidental errors. We would be happy to apply the corrections in the following edition of this publication.